PRAISE FOR THE VAGABONDING WITH KIDS SERIES

"A thrilling trek through the Amazonian rain forest and a vibrant read about the adventures of being a vagabonding family."
—Lisa Ferland, *Knocked Up Abroad*

"AK Turner keeps it real in *Vagabonding with Kids: Brazil*, an entertaining snapshot of family life on the road that speaks to the traveler, the parent, the adventurer."
—Rob Taylor, 2TravelDads

"AK Turner shares what many of us only dream of, traveling the world with children. While it's not romanticized as being challenge-free, she shares a life experience interlaced with humorous moments that make many of us believe our dreams are actually within reach . . . if we can just take that first step."
—Jim Pickell, President, HomeExchange.com

"Refreshing, honest, and humorous. I couldn't put it down!"
—Vicky Etherington, *Eat Sleep Love Travel*

"A hilarious and uncensored adventure—Turner's stories of family travel go from cute as a koala bear to crazy as a Tasmanian devil faster than your kids can say, 'Are we there yet?'"
—Susanne Kerns, *The Dusty Parachute*

"Capturing the real face of family travel—the laughs, anxiety, and adjustments—*Vagabonding with Kids: Australia* takes you on the trip of a lifetime to the land Down Under. A brilliant read for all parents, travelers, and wanderlusters."

—Alyson Long, *World Travel Family*

". . . a rollicking, outrageous, hilarious adventure. Buckle up!"

—Michelle Newman, *You're My Favorite Today*

"Adventurous, funny, and inspirational, this book will convince you that traveling with kids isn't impossible. It's irresistible."

—Karen Alpert, *New York Times* bestselling author of *I Heart My Little A-Holes* and *I Want My Epidural Back*

"Everyone dreams of escaping the 9-to-5, but few have the guts to actually do it. AK dares to live her life on purpose and has realized early in life that true riches aren't reflected in accumulated possessions but are the vast and unique experiences we collect. If you're ready to dive into the digital nomad lifestyle, you must read this book. AK proves anyone can do it—even a family!"

—Christy Hovey, *The 9-to-5 Escape Artist: A Startup Guide for Aspiring Lifestyle Entrepreneurs and Digital Nomads*

Vagabonding
with kids
ALASKA

ALSO BY AK TURNER

VAGABONDING WITH KIDS SERIES

Vagabonding with Kids
Vagabonding with Kids: Australia
Vagabonding with Kids: Brazil

TALES OF IMPERFECTION SERIES

This Little Piggy Went to the Liquor Store
Mommy Had a Little Flask
Hair of the Corn Dog

Vagabonding
with kids
ALASKA

AK TURNER

Vagabonding with Kids: Alaska

Brown Books Publishing Group
16250 Knoll Trail Drive, Suite 205
Dallas, Texas 75248
www.BrownBooks.com
(972) 381-0009

A New Era in Publishing®

Library of Congress Cataloging-in-Publication Data

Names: Turner, A. K. (Amanda K.), author.
Title: Vagabonding with kids : Alaska : sea lions aren't cuddly and other
    truths of the last frontier / AK Turner.
Other titles: Vagabonding with kids Alaska | Sea lions aren't cuddly and other
    truths of the last frontier
Description: Dallas : Brown Books Pub. Group, [2017] | Series: Vagabonding
    with kids ; 4
Identifiers: LCCN 2017019385 | ISBN 9781612549767 (pbk.)
Subjects: LCSH: Alaska--Description and travel. | Turner family. | Children--
    Travel--Alaska--Humor. | Alaska--Social life and customs--Anecdotes.
Classification: LCC F910.5 .T87 2017 | DDC 917.9804--dc23

ISBN 978-1-61254-976-7
LCCN 2017019385

Printed in the United States
10 9 8 7 6 5 4 3 2 1

Design by Sarah Tregay, DesignWorks Creative, Inc.
Cover Photo by Mike Turner

For more information or to contact the author, please go to
VagabondingWithKids.com or AKTurner.com.

For my favorite Alaskan.
You know who you are.

(Alaska state flag)

 ★ Juneau

○ Sitka

ALASKA

○ Ketchikan

○ Prince Rupert

BRITISH COLUMBIA

ALBERTA

Vanderhoof ○   ○ Prince George

Valemount ○   ○ Jasper

○ Banff

Radium Hot Springs ○

○ Bonner's Ferry
○ Sandpoint
○ Farragut

Winchester ○

● Boise

IDAHO

N

PACIFIC OCEAN

CONTENTS

Scat

Paranoia is just having the right information.

—William S. Burroughs

I stepped over the largest pile of dog poop I'd ever seen, what looked to be a twelve-pound Hershey's kiss of excrement, and contemplated the stupidity of the previous ten minutes. We'd disembarked to the island from a small, lurching boat, and I'd handed my two-month-old daughter over the side.

"It's fine," my husband had assured me, reaching for Emilia. I looked at his footing, balanced on slippery rocks peeking out of the water. "I've got her. Don't worry."

When we'd reached the island, the light rain thickened. On semisolid, sandy ground, I took Emilia from Mike so that he and his father could secure the boat. And with my daughter in my arms, I felt the unmistakable heft of a loaded diaper.

"Oh, crap," I said.

"What's wrong?" my mother-in-law asked, but then she

figured it out before I had a chance to answer. "Oh. You mean crap. Literally."

"Yes," I confirmed. "I don't know why I didn't check her diaper before we got off. The floor of the boat would have been better than this." A rainy beach is a less-than-ideal setting in which to change a child's diaper. I spied a large rock and chalked it up as my best bet, placing a blanket underneath my daughter.

"I can at least try to shield you a bit from the rain," my mother-in-law offered. The diaper change involved the usual actions, along with removing and replacing Emilia's fluffy bear cub outfit. "Dress warm," my in-laws had advised, and this was the warmest thing she had. I'm not sure if it was meant to be pajamas or a Halloween costume or both, but it served well as a means of keeping two-month-old Emilia insulated from the cold.

I'm all for a good hike, always in favor of combining exercise, fresh air, and scenery. The hour-and-a-half journey to reach the island, the rain, the uncertainty of handing my baby over the side of the boat, and the act of changing her diaper on a rock, however, amassed into beginning the hike on the wrong foot. And what should have been fresh air reeked of dung.

Kruzof is a 167-square-mile island in the Alexander Archipelago of Southeast Alaska and is typically accessed by boat or floatplane from the nearby town of Sitka, located ten miles to the east. Like most places in North America, Kruzof has cycled through a handful of names. The Tlingit, Spanish, French, and British called it Tlikh, San Jacinto, St. Hyacinthe, and Pitt, respectively. Various Russians named it Sitka Island, Crooze, and Edgecumbe. This last moniker was due to the presence on the island of Mount Edgecumbe, a small, dormant volcano. And I was afraid of it.

The descriptors of "small" and "dormant" do nothing to lessen my fears of volcanoes. Plenty of "small" volcanoes loom large enough to dwarf cities and are still conduits for Mother Nature's terrifying forces. And as for "dormant," I only had to hear the phrase "previously thought to be dormant" once to render the word discredited as far as I was concerned. (Six years after our visit, an eleven-year-old Sitkan exploring Kruzof with his family would find a burnt tree embedded in pumice. Geologists descended upon the find, and analysis revealed it to be an ancient Sitka spruce—more than thirteen thousand years old—charred from one of Edgecumbe's eruptions.[1])

My father-in-law led the hike along a slight trail, made narrower by the large piles of poop one had to dodge every few feet. My husband followed, with Emilia strapped to his chest in a carrier. My mother-in-law and I trailed behind. We were a quiet group. The others seemed in good spirits about hiking in the rain on a volcanic island, while I tried to come up with a plan if the "dormant" volcano switched to the "previously thought to be dormant" variety.

A year prior, I might not have dwelled on possible catastrophes. I might have gladly tromped through the rain, viewing the outing as adventurous, but as it was, I was a new mother and just then realizing that along with motherhood comes the constant necessity to manage one's fear and guilt. Parents keep this a closely guarded secret from parents-to-be, as if they want to lure us into the club with Rockwellian images so that we might unknowingly enter a state of fear and guilt comparable to their own. As we hiked on a volcanic island in the rain with a two-month-old, through terrain that looked as if a herd of cattle with loose bowels had recently traversed it, my fear and guilt were firmly in check.

I bumped into my husband, who'd abruptly stopped in front of me.

"What's wrong? Why'd you stop?" I asked.

"Shh." He motioned to his father up ahead.

My father-in-law was holding up his rifle in full shooter stance, aimed in the direction of thick forest. I'm sure "shooter stance" would cause my gun aficionado friends a roll of the eyes and a good chuckle, but that's how I thought of it. He stood still, in such quiet that I instinctively held my breath. How had I not noticed the presence of a rifle? Were we supposed to hunt along the hike? Would I be expected to assist in the "packing out" of a deer? Would my father-in-law try to teach me how to field dress an animal? I'd heard him speak of such things, and they generally began with the phrase, "So, you start cutting at the asshole, and you work your way up."

Surely not.

As we stood there waiting, for either gunfire or an explanation, I looked at my feet. Yet another pile of excrement, fairly fresh, sat in the middle of the trail like misplaced punctuation. Of course, no herd of cattle roamed Kruzof Island. I tried to picture hikers ahead of us, accompanied by a fair number of monstrous dogs, all of which inexplicably shared the same intestinal distress. Even this unlikelihood could not account for the amount of poop around us. In that moment, waiting for the shot to ring out, I admitted what I'd been so desperate to deny. There were no cows or dogs, and this was not a hunting trip.

We were in Alaska.

We were in bear country.

My father-in-law remained with his rifle raised. I waited for a beast to charge from the trees. I looked to Mike and our daughter dressed as a cub strapped to his chest. The rain fell harder, and my anger manifested itself in silent tears. Another moment passed before my father-in-law casually lowered his rifle. He looked at the rest of us, still frozen in place, and said, "Oh, I was just using the scope to look around."

I gritted my teeth to the point of aching jaw.

We continued hiking in the rain across the bear-infested island while I silently fumed. Mike tried a few times to ask me what was wrong, and I managed through hot tears little more than, "This is stupid" and "I hate this" and "I don't want to talk about it," which he knows is code for "Only later will I unleash my wrath in all its terrifying glory."

I realized why my husband and in-laws had been uncharacteristically silent at the outset. They hadn't wanted to acknowledge the startling amount of bear scat along the trail, lest they alarm me. As if the scat itself wouldn't scare the scat out of me once I finally admitted the reality of the situation.

Trekking quietly through bear country is not the best course of action. Tips on bear safety involve making noise, thought to deter bears and limit the chance of surprising them. It's not common for bears to attack humans, but it happens nonetheless, along with occasional cases of bears *stalking* humans. No matter how rare these instances are, their existence is much like the "previously thought to be dormant" volcano. "Normal" bear behavior is no longer relevant, because there's always an exception.

Bears have a wildly diverse diet. Sure, this includes fish and berries, but they've also been recorded as having consumed over a hundred different species of mammal. There'd be no reason for them to exclude from the menu a pouting woman still carrying some tasty baby weight.

The peak of the hike was intended to be when we reached the other side of the island, where we met up with a few friends who'd come out earlier in the day. By that time, I'd managed to stop crying, though I still viewed the entire outing as ludicrous—a postpartum nightmare of bad decisions and proof that not only would we fail as parents, we'd fail hard and early.

Was this genuinely terrible or was it just me? Was everyone else having a really good time? Was this a normal day of enjoying the Alaskan outdoors? And were there other activities that I viewed as distasteful but which Alaskans really enjoyed? Maybe after hiking in rainy, bear-infested woods, we would all go contract lice together and try to cultivate hangnails.

The intent of the day was to enjoy the beach overlooking Shelikof Bay, which might have been possible if not for the weather. Instead we exchanged brief pleasantries with our friends before beginning the return trek.

The hike was a little over two hours. We were slowed by slippery terrain, the accompaniment of a two-month-old baby, and my pissy attitude, which was likely half-circumstantial and half-hormonal. We then had another hour and a half on the boat to return to the town of Sitka. I was wet, cold, and uncomfortable physically and emotionally.

It was also our eighth wedding anniversary.

* * *

Sitka is a popular town in Southeast Alaska, with residents numbering around nine thousand but tourists aplenty.

When the cruise ships are in, the tiny downtown is crowded and does a swift business in souvenirs. Others come by plane or ferry for the "Alaska experience," the definition of which depends on your interests. Many leave with great, insulated fish boxes, filled with salmon, halibut, lingcod, and rockfish. Others take guided mountain goat hunting tours, killing the animals that bear no resemblance to the type of goat that is fashionable as a pet but instead weigh up to three hundred pounds and have beautiful long white coats. Many visitors list Sitka on their itineraries with no intention to harvest or hunt but rather to enjoy the beauty of Sitka, to kayak among the smattering of surrounding islands, and to lose track of how many bald eagles they've spotted in a single afternoon.

Our trip to Sitka was more of a homecoming than tourist venture. It had been nine years since we'd visited the town where my husband was born and raised. The ill-fated hike across Kruzof wasn't the only negative of our trip. As a new, breastfeeding mother, I contracted mastitis, but what trip is complete without a painful breast infection? Mike was also eager to reconnect with high school buddies and one night relived his youth by playing video games at a friend's house until dawn. I spent the night in a hotel room with Emilia, feeling abandoned and wondering if this was his way of saying that he wanted a divorce. *He changed his mind*, I thought. *Now that we have a kid and he realizes how much work it is and that he can't binge on* Assassin's Creed, *he wants out. Damn the advancement of technology in the gaming world! If I were just up against* Ms. Pac-Man, *I might have had a chance. Single motherhood, here I come.*

Of course, that wasn't the case, and Mike simply wanted to see friends he hadn't seen in years, but in my already fragile physical and emotional state, that's what I concluded.

On the plane ride home, I gave voice to my hurt feelings, which accounted for a near constant state of tension and an unbecoming vein pulsating in my forehead. Mike assured me that everything was fine, apologized for staying out so late, and suggested that perhaps it was okay if we didn't spend every waking and at-rest moment together. This thinking lasted until I broached the subject of doing something fun without him, at which point he wondered why I wouldn't want to spend every waking and at-rest moment together. In any case, we survived the trip with both our lives and marriage intact, but I left with no desire to return in the near future.

I'd have nine years to gear up for the next trip. I'd bring my A game, a positive attitude, my six- and nine-year-old daughters, and plenty of bear spray.

* * *

Onward

When planning a trip to Alaska, one must first decide how to get there. Flying seems a straightforward option, unless you end up with a plane that at the last moment before touchdown veers up suddenly and announces that landing in Sitka will not be possible. This happened to me on my first Alaskan adventure, while traveling alone and before I'd met my husband. The pilot diverted to Juneau, Alaska's capital city (though people in the Lower 48 often guess Anchorage or Fairbanks), where I spent a night at a nearby Travelodge before the plane made a second and more successful attempt the following day.

Sitka's Rocky Gutierrez Airport is located on Japonski Island and connected to town by the two-lane, cable-stayed John O'Connell Bridge spanning the Sitka Channel. Before completion of the bridge in 1971, Sitkans and tourists had to commute by ferry to the airport, which I can only imagine heightened the anxiety of already-harried travelers. In the nearby town of Ketchikan, a short ferry ride is *still* required to access the airport. Maybe this isn't that big of a deal in practice, but I imagine that when more than one mode of transport is required to leave town, you feel an added level of stress. Running late would put you in danger of not only missing your flight but also missing your boat, causing you to miss your flight. It's an increase in the potential for failure.

Sitka's Japonski Island is a small blot of land and home to a lone runway surrounded by water on three sides. Add to this the ever-unpredictable weather and wind gusts off the water, and you can imagine why every now and then a pilot makes the call that conditions may not be suitable. Of the dozens of flights my husband has made to Sitka throughout his life, he's never experienced this diversion, while it happened to me on my first try. I'm just lucky, I guess.

The other means of accessing Sitka is through the Alaska Marine Highway ferry system, which can be done with or without a vehicle. We planned our trip when our daughters were six and nine years of age. They were well traveled by that point and for the most part enjoyed one another's company without endless refrains of "I know you are, but what am I?" We felt they might be at the age when a road trip with them could be described without the word *excruciating*.

We settled on driving through northern Idaho into Canada and boarding the Alaska Marine Highway ferry in Prince Rupert, British Columbia. From there we'd have a day and a half aboard the ferry before reaching Sitka. Though far more expensive than flying to Sitka, the road trip and ferry would allow us to have our vehicle during our month-long stay in Alaska and give us the added adventure of road tripping through northern Idaho and Canada.

Before we'd made it thirty miles from our home in Boise, Mike began sneezing.

"Here, I've got lots of tissues," I said, shoving them at him.

"Where are the allergy pills? Do you have the allergy pills?"

"Right here." I gave him two pills and a water bottle. "Do you want me to drive?" I asked.

"No, I'm fine."

"Well, let me know. Driving while sneezing is dangerous."

I envisioned the headline: "Sneeze Plummets Ill-Fated Road Trippers off Cliff."

"Are those pills?" six-year-old Ivy asked from the backseat. "I love pills."

It should be noted here that my six-year-old did not have an affinity for swallowing pills or the aftereffects of doing so. She was, however, proud of her ability to take a pill while her older sister struggled with it, and she turned this pride into a professed beloved pastime. The ease or difficulty with which my daughters ingest pills was revealed before a trip to Brazil and by means of an oral typhoid vaccine. Ever since, Ivy has been quick to point out how much she loves pills, while Emilia continues to have a hard time with them.

"Well, I just hate swallowing," said Emilia, sensing her sister's one-upmanship.

"Are you serious?" asked Ivy. "Swallowing is my favorite part."

Mike shot me a sidelong glance from the driver's seat. No part of the backseat conversation was what any parent wants to hear from their children.

"Well," Emilia reconsidered. "I like swallowing but only when things are squishy and go down my throat."

"Mom," Ivy called. "I'm hungry."

"Great," I said, eager for a change in conversation. "Because we're going to stop in McCall for breakfast."

It seemed odd to set out on a sizable adventure and make our first stop after only a few hours, but that's the difference between road tripping with and without kids. Children necessitate more breaks. They have shorter attention spans, greater appetites, and smaller bladders.

The drive from Boise to McCall is two hours through one hundred miles of scenic byway that snakes along the Payette River. The town of McCall has a population of around three thousand, but the former logging community is now a year-round resort town drawing tourists in numbers that far exceed the residents. It's popular to play on Payette Lake in the summer to relieve the Idaho heat. In the winter, tourists flock for the Winter Carnival, with everything from snow sculptures to comedy shows to snowbike races. There's also the draw of skiing, of course. At nearby Brundage or Tamarack, or at McCall's own Little Ski Hill, people can engage in that odd compulsion to slide down a snowy decline at unadvisable speeds.

As we parked outside of the Fogglifter Café, Ivy asked, "Are we still in Idaho?"

"We sure are," Mike confirmed.

"Oh." Her shoulders slumped in disappointment.

After breakfast, we lingered at the café, and the girls read books while Mike and I checked our e-mail. We'd made it a full two hours into our summer-long trip before allowing ourselves to be sucked back into the virtual world.

"Are you about ready to get back on the road?" I asked.

"Since we're here, why don't we take a little walk down by the lake before we head out," he suggested.

We did so, stopping to take a picture at McCall's water-front sundial. By standing on the square corresponding to the current month, a shadow is cast toward an outer circle of numbers, indicating the time of day. Sundials date back thousands of years, to ancient Egyptian and Babylonian astronomy. To me, that's sufficient evidence that freakishly smart people have been around much longer than we tend to think. Figuring out how to tell time using the sun can't be easy, but they had to because there was a documented shortage of iPhones in 1500 BC.

When we got back on the road, it felt as if the trip truly began. We'd been in McCall a dozen times before, so going beyond the resort town signified a journey into new territory.

The landscape in Idaho varies from rolling hills to jagged peaks to flattened plains. It is a state of rivers, wild, forested mountains, and high desert speckled with sagebrush. We drove north to Whitebird, and I couldn't help but mutter a series of less-than-eloquent phrases like "Wow" and "It's so pretty," until we crested a summit that gave way to the Camas Prairie, and the previously dynamic scenery melted into monotony.

"What were you saying about the view?" Mike said.

"Well, it *was* pretty."

By the time we reached Coeur d'Alene, we'd traveled for over seven hours and were ready to stop. I'd heard a lot about Coeur d'Alene from friends who enjoy it as a go-to getaway. It's a city of only about fifty thousand people but with a steady tourist industry due to Lake Coeur d'Alene and resorts that capitalize on it, much like McCall. It speaks to the basic human instinct to seek out water. People flock to coasts when they can; when landlocked, they seek out lakes and rivers.

"Let's go down by the water," Mike suggested. From a distance, Coeur d'Alene's City Beach beckoned. Sunbathers crowded along narrow stretches of sand. Towering trees shaded an adjacent park and playground.

"It looks popular," I said.

"Can we go in the water?" Emilia asked.

"I'm not sure," I answered, "but we can check it out."

"Are we still in Idaho?" Ivy asked.

"Still in Idaho," Mike confirmed.

"Idaho takes forever," she lamented.

Close encounters with City Beach revealed it to be less attractive than we'd first thought. An abundance of people smoked, spat periodically, and willfully littered their beer cans. In my late teens or early twenties, I might have felt at home in such surroundings, but that was many years ago.

"So, it's kind of gross here," I said, silently acknowledging that in my late teens and early twenties, I was kind of gross.

"Yes," Mike admitted. He will deny a great deal of unsavoriness to spend time near sand and water, but the Coeur d'Alene beach on that afternoon was too much for even him. I know that what we experienced was not typical of Coeur d'Alene, as my friends who love CDA, as it's known, would have also found the beach off-putting on that particular day. We'd unfortunately stumbled onto City Beach when it hosted an anomalous crowd of disrespectful youth. Again, one could easily argue I resembled them at that age, but that doesn't change the fact that the current me has no desire to hang out with my younger self.

"Let's go into town instead," I suggested.

Strolling along Sherman Avenue in downtown Coeur d'Alene, we stumbled upon Figpickels Toy Emporium.

"Can we go in there?" Emilia gasped.

"Please please please please please please please!" Ivy added.

"Okay," I said. "But we are not going to buy anything. Do you understand? We can look around, but we are not going to buy anything."

In Figpickels Toy Emporium, I wanted to buy everything. Topping my list was a lava lamp in which the "lava" took the form of a jellyfish. I really felt I needed it and that somehow it would vastly improve the quality of my life. Unfortunately, there was more than one hitch to my potential ownership of a jellyfish lava lamp. First, if I purchased anything, I would lose all credibility in the eyes of my children, and they'd learn firsthand the meaning of hypocrisy.

I was actually okay with that.

The greater impediment was space. We had a packed truck, and it was only day one of our summer-long adventure. Buying a lamp would not be the most prudent decision. I went through various scenarios in my head. I could hold the lamp on my lap, and we could plug it in at each stop along the way. And then I felt I truly identified with Steve Martin's character in *The Jerk*, at which point I knew it was time to let it go.

Figpickels also had a moving, six-foot Ferris wheel replica and a working, three-horsed carousel, which we let the girls ride for a quarter. Employees demonstrated toys and games for us as we browsed, and somehow, against all odds, we left only having spent the quarter for the carousel. (I still want the lamp.)

Our one overnight stop in Idaho before venturing into Canada was at Farragut State Park. We stayed in a cabin, which thankfully didn't include any of the things that come to my mind when I think of a cabin, like black widows and bed bugs and serial killers whose preferred accessories are hatchets. The most dangerous things we encountered at Farragut were the ground squirrel burrows. These hidden holes in the earth were potential ankle breakers during the hours we spent kicking around a partially deflated soccer ball. Though I'll take ground squirrels over serial killers any day.

"Maybe while we're here we should record a podcast," Mike suggested.

We'd recently assisted Emilia in creating her own podcast of five-minute interviews with people we meet during our travels. While my eldest struggles to relate to kids her own age, she has no problem speaking with adults, nor does she shy away from a microphone.

"Ooh, maybe a park ranger," said Emilia. "That would be cool."

At the ranger station, we met Ranger Kim, who was amenable to the idea. Emilia began by asking Kim about her job. Kim explained that she checked campers in and sold them ice, snacks, and retail items.

"Oh. So wait," Emilia said. "Your job is what?" At which point Kim patiently repeated her duties. Kim later revealed that she owned five horses.

"You own five horses?" Emilia gasped.

"Yes, five horses."

"So what are their names?"

"Their names are Major, Sunny, Red, Max, and Tug," answered Kim.

"Oh, so you have how many horses?"

My main goal during these podcasts is to remain still and silent in the background, with an intense look on my face as if I'm witnessing Pulitzer Prize–winning journalism in action. There are times when I have to put a hand over my mouth to hide a smile, because I know that the second Emilia sees me trying not to laugh, she won't want to continue the endeavor.

We took advantage of the park's amenities before continuing our journey north, including a few hours at Beaver Bay Beach on the southwest tip of Lake Pend Oreille (pronounced Pond Oray). The mountain of cargo we hauled in the bed of our pickup truck included an inflatable paddleboard, which we thought might be put to use along the journey as well as when we reached Alaska. While Mike and Emilia paddled around the lake, I sat on shore as Ivy stood in two feet of water. Another family nestled into a spot a few yards down the beach.

"Mom?" Ivy asked loudly. "Can I pee in this water?"

"Um, yes, Ivy. But you don't have to shout. I'm right here; I can hear you."

Ivy moved into a telling squat with no sign of discretion and in an even louder voice said, "Oh, that feels so good."

Moving on from Farragut, we drove along Highway 95 toward Sandpoint, Idaho. Bumper stickers along the way trashed vegetarians, displayed Confederate flags, and asserted that Donald Trump would make America great again. These elements were tempered when we passed a large building with a sign that read simply, "Hippie Store."

The marker for knowing you're almost to Sandpoint has nothing to do with politics or lifestyle and is instead Sandpoint's Long Bridge. The two-mile span over Lake Pend

Oreille delivers travelers to the hamlet once named by both Rand McNally and *USA Today* as America's "Most Beautiful Small Town."

Unable to pass by a beach area without checking it out, Mike pulled in at Sandpoint's main beach, and we extracted beach blankets and snacks from the cooler with the intent to enjoy the water for a bit before the bulk of the day's driving. At one point, a neighboring group, including a middle-aged father and two children, lost a plastic bag. A gust of wind swooped the bag into the air, and Mike dove to catch it as it passed by our blanket, but the bag flew by, farther down the beach.

The owner of the bag looked over. "Was that mine?" he asked.

"I think so," I replied. "My husband tried to get it but missed."

I expected him to stand and hurry to retrieve his trash. Instead, he shrugged with an apathetic "huh" and watched it bounce and blow through the park.

Don't you know this is our nation's Most Beautiful Small Town? I thought. *You should be hauling ass!* Then I wondered if I should just haul ass, but the bag had already been swept away and out of sight.

I wondered if the plastic bag would eventually make it to the sea, despite its Idaho origins. If so, would it devastate some poor sea creature? Would it choke a sea turtle that mistook it for a jellyfish? I hoped instead that it would somehow make it into the plumbing system and cause an incredible overflow of a toilet belonging to the bag's owner, in a grand display of environmental karma.

Our last stop before crossing the border into Canada was in Bonner's Ferry, Idaho. With each previous stop, the towns had become smaller, and Bonner's Ferry settled on the border with just a few thousand people but a history similar to many other Idaho cities.

The town legacy included the usual suspects of fur trading, mining, logging, and, of course, mishandling Native American relations. The Kootenai tribe had been decimated and largely ignored by the Bureau of Indian Affairs, which contested that the tribe was too small to warrant further assistance. The Kootenai were relegated to decayed homes without bathing facilities. In the early 1970s, Tribal Council chairwoman Amy Trice checked on an elder only to find that he'd frozen to death in his unheated home. She responded by declaring war on the United States of America. The Kootenai means of carrying out war was to place ten-cent tolls at each end of the town; this was the price to pay for traveling through the lands that had been taken from them. The money collected would be used for elder care. Though many were sympathetic, tensions heightened when state police arrived to end the "conflict." Within a few weeks, the US government granted the tribe a concession and land grant, and Trice's efforts are credited with saving the Bonner's Ferry Kootenai from extinction, alleviating their poverty, and setting the tribe on the path to economic independence. I met Amy Trice in 2010, a year before her death, and seeing Bonner's Ferry for the first time gave me a window into the setting for this unique and little-known event in Idaho's history.

"This town is small," I noted. "And so quiet."

"Let's just get a quick bite to eat," said Mike. He circled around a block in what would have constituted downtown. "Although this seems to be a town without restaurants."

"I'm sure if we drive around, we'll find something," I said.

At which point we drove around in circles, passing closed businesses with taxidermy animals in the windows, and no sign of an eating establishment. Bonner's Ferry is a town of only two and a half square miles. Restaurants were not in abundance.

"Let me check my phone," said Mike. After a brief search, he proclaimed, "I got one!"

He parked the car in front of a closed accounting business with a large stuffed cougar in the window.

"I don't think this place has food," said Ivy.

"Maybe they serve mountain lion," Emilia ventured.

"It's just around the corner," said Mike.

And around the corner we discovered a tiny restaurant called Soulshine. The name and décor and menu indicated that Soulshine was a place of peace, love, and gigantic burritos. The antithesis of every Confederate flag decal I'd seen, it was a restaurant with its heart on its sleeve, which I thought might be a difficult thing to be in northern Idaho. The proprietor could not have been more welcoming and generous, sending us off with good vibrations and free chocolate-chip cookies. We would depart our home state and truly begin our journey with nothing on our minds but sweet kindness.

* * *

O Canada

*I'm kinda disappointed that Canada isn't
like the* South Park *movie said it was.*

—Joel Madden

At security checkpoints, I become irrationally nervous. Despite being a tedious rule follower with no illegal hobbies, the process of showing documents and declaring that I'm not doing anything wrong makes my heart race and my upper lip sweat. Crossing the border into Canada, I held our passports at the ready and was prepared to answer all potential questions, which I had researched online ahead of time so that I could practice my answers and try not to sound like a liar.

After a mere two minutes of fessing up to how much alcohol we had and declaring our bear spray, we were let through.

"Wow." I exhaled in relief. "She didn't even interrogate the kids."

"Why would she interrogate the kids?" Mike asked.

"Because that's what they do when you take kids across borders. They make kids answer questions to expose the bad people pretending to be good parents."

"You think we look like bad people pretending to be good parents?"

"Of course! You can't judge someone by how they look. Think of Ted Bundy!"

"Do I have to? Hey, look at the water."

I thought he was changing the subject because he knows that once I mention a serial killer, I'm likely to continue in that vein for hours, but then I turned to look at the river adjacent to the road. The water glowed.

"Oh my gosh, it's beautiful," I agreed.

"It looks Photoshopped," Mike added.

"What are you guys talking about?" Emilia asked from the backseat, and I was glad Mike had diverted our conversation from child trafficking and serial killers.

"Look at how beautiful it is. Look at the water," Mike said. "It's so *bright*."

"Wow," said Ivy. "Canada's awesome."

"Yeah," Emilia agreed. "I really love it here." We'd been in Canada for two minutes, but apparently it agreed with her.

"Hey, Emilia," Ivy said. "I've got a joke. What do you call a granola bar that doesn't cost very much? Chocolate *cheap*."

"That's a good one, Ivy," I said.

"Well, I've got one, too," Emilia said. "It has the same answer. What type of cookie does a tweety bird like?" To Emilia, a *tweety bird* is a type of bird.

"Uh, chocolate cheep?" Ivy guessed.

"Good job. You figured it out," said Emilia.

"That's because you told me the answer before the joke."

"Yeah but still. Here's another one. What is a toilet's favorite flavor? *Pee*-nut *butt*-er. Do you get it?"

"Didn't you girls say you were going to nap or something?" I called, hoping to put an end to the potty humor.

"I have an idea," Mike said. "Let's do a round robin of 'Canada.'" He then bellowed "Canada" in a baritone, holding the final a.

I followed suit, then Emilia, and finally Ivy, until we were all singing the last a, holding the note as long as we could until on the verge of passing out. We would randomly continue to do this throughout Canada. We continued the round robin with "Alaska" when we reached our destination. It was a prime example of the fact that we are unafraid of intense levels of dorkdom, a state in which we feel the need to revel as much as possible before our daughters become teenagers, when there is a greater possibility that they will refuse to engage in such behavior.

Each mile (I mean, kilometer) that brought us closer to Banff was more beautiful that the last. Snowcapped mountains loomed, filtering down into picturesque streams of bright blue and green. We spotted dozens of deer along the way, as exciting the twentieth time as it was the first.

"The mountains here are amazing," I said.

"Can we stop and maybe climb one of them?" Emilia asked.

"I don't think so."

"Besides," Mike added, "we want to get to Banff. It's Canada Day!"

"Cool," said Emilia.

"Maybe they'll have a parade," Ivy ventured.

"I don't think they're going to have a parade," I said, not wanting to get her hopes up.

"Actually," Mike corrected, "there will be a parade."

"Oh, well there you go. Except we just passed a sign that says the exit for Banff is closed."

"What do you mean the exit is closed? How are we supposed to get there?"

"It's probably because of the parade," I guessed. "But it said the exit is closed as of 4:30."

We looked at the clock on the dash. It read 4:26. Mike stepped on the gas. We made the exit but then came to a standstill in traffic within Banff as crowds of people and lines of cars descended on the town to celebrate Canada Day. We checked in to the Buffalo Mountain Lodge, a hotel pricier than our usual accommodations but the only one available in light of the holiday. By the grace of the hotel shuttle, we arrived downtown just in time to watch the parade. I was coaching my girls through the disappointment of not being able to see very well, as throngs of people had staked out their spots long before our arrival, when a woman kindly let Emilia and Ivy horn in on her space. They had prime seats to watch a group of Filipino Canadians, a troupe of Polish dancers, and imaginative floats that served as ads for tour companies and gondola rides. The parade ended, and the girls gobbled candy given out by parade participants.

"Canada is so awesome," Ivy said. "I love it here."

It was by chance that we arrived at our first destination in Canada on Canada Day; as a result, my daughters believed that Canada was a place of not only mountains and wildlife but also parades and free candy. I had no reason to tell them otherwise.

Banff was beyond lovely, the type of resort town that lulls me in with shops and restaurants and endless photo ops and reminds me that I will never be able to afford to live in such a place. We visited the Banff Park Museum, a trove of natural history and a ridiculous amount of taxidermy housed in a log cabin, circa 1903. At the Buffalo Nations Luxton Museum, we learned about the culture of the First Nations indigenous groups and the devastation to their populations once the white man muscled in. This led to Emilia's repeated question of why people are so rude, to which I have never settled on a satisfactory answer.

* * *

"You are my favorite person in the world," Mike whispered. This is something we say to one another often. It's a romantic little reassurance that after two decades together, we are still committed to our relationship and each other. He said these words as we packed up to leave Banff and at the exact moment that a mosquito landed on the wall beside his head.

Like most warm-blooded creatures, I'm not a fan of mosquitos. In response to his romantic gesture, I screamed, "Mosquito!" and slapped the wall next to his head, leaving a blight of blood and crushed insect where the bug had perched a second before. "I mean, I love you, too."

Talk of Banff eventually leads to Lake Louise, a glacial lake forty minutes outside of Banff and an often-touted, must-see stop along Alberta's section of the Trans-Canada Highway. Our driving time for the day was only a few hours, as we wanted to spend a night or two in Jasper before pushing hard on the remainder of our journey to reach Prince Rupert and the Alaska Marine Highway. I imagined we'd spend a few hours at Lake Louise, perhaps breaking out the paddleboard.

"Does everyone have their bathing suits on under their clothes?" I asked. The weather in Banff had been warm, not terribly different from the heat of summer in Idaho.

"Will we get to go swimming?" Emilia asked.

"Probably not," I answered. "It is a glacial lake, but if we go paddleboarding, you'll want to have your suit on." I donned shorts, a T-shirt, and flip-flops, and we loaded everything and everyone into the truck.

Forty minutes later, I was sure we'd made a terrible mistake. We sat in an interminable line of cars inching along a one-lane road, which we assumed would lead to the lake.

"Are we sure we even want to do this?" I asked.

"Well it's not as if I can turn around now," said Mike.

"I think we're coming up on the parking lot." I pointed ahead, where brightly vested people directed traffic. We drove into a packed lot, and the traffic directors immediately waved us to the exit, so that we found ourselves leaving, without ever having seen the lake.

"What?! This is ridiculous," Mike fumed.

"Let's just go," I suggested.

"No. I do not accept that." He made the last possible turn back into the parking lot before we'd have been funneled back out to the highway.

"But there aren't any parking spaces."

"There's one," he said, and against all odds, he slipped the pickup into a recently vacated spot.

"Wow. Good job persevering. I would have bailed a long time ago."

"I know, sweetie," he said. "That's why I usually drive."

Our elation at having found a space dissipated as soon as

we opened the doors. My instructions to have the girls wear their bathing suits under their clothes now seemed ludicrous.

"Okay, so everyone needs to get a jacket," I said.

I was terribly underdressed in my shorts and flip-flops but noticed other groups of tourists in the same predicament. The wind picked up, and our foursome huddled close as we followed a path leading from the parking lot to the lake.

The waters of Lake Louise, like the waters of the rivers we'd admired since entering Canada, had a bright turquoise hue, almost iridescent, caused by silt-sized rock particles carried down from the glacier overlooking the lake. Flocks of people took pictures, smiling and shivering in the cold.

"Can we do that?" Emilia asked. She pointed to a dock from which the adventurous disembarked on rented canoes.

"No," Mike and I chimed.

"Why not?" Ivy whined.

"Because it costs money," Mike said, still feeling the sting of the Banff hotel bill and the dread of many expenses yet to come.

"And it's so cold," I said. "Can we go now?" The beauty of the lake and surrounding mountains was undeniable, but so was the chattering of my teeth.

The drive to Jasper included endless directions from Mike to "Take a picture now. Wait, take another one right now. Oh, take a picture of that mountain. Are you getting all of this?"

"I've taken exactly five hundred million pictures. Okay?" I said.

"Mom," Ivy called from the backseat. "I think you might be lying."

"I've taken a lot of fantastic pictures," I assured Mike.

"I can't help it," he said. "It's like every second there's

another incredible view."

Anyone who has traveled the Icefields Parkway through the Canadian Rocky Mountains understands this compulsion, and the drive between Banff and Jasper is considered one of the loveliest in the world. With plenty of turnouts to stop and photograph glaciers, lakes, and mountains, the journey took much longer than the three and a half hours the GPS predicted; there was a lot of oohing and ahhing to be done along the way.

A change in weather during the latter half of the drive gave me a reprieve from constant photographing. The cold but sunny day clouded over, and light rain turned into heavy downpour. Because we traveled on routes within Banff and Jasper National Parks, we saw no signs of commerce. Winding on narrow roads up mountains in increasingly inclement weather had me wondering just how long we could survive on what we had with us (four hot-dog buns, half a bag of tortilla chips, and a dozen cans of beer), should the situation turn dire.

With our arrival in Jasper came a welcome respite from the weather, as well as relief at the sight of a town with gas stations and grocery stores. After a quick glance at the town of Jasper and a stop to refuel, lest we again find ourselves traveling for hundreds of miles with no sign of a gas station, we curved our way up a small road headed for Patricia Lake Bungalows, where we'd booked a one-room cabin.

"It should be just another few miles up ahead," I said.

"Yes, but it looks like traffic is about to stop."

We came to a stop behind four other cars in the middle of a stretch of road bordered by trees. My first thought was of ducks or geese crossing the road, because that would have been the cause for a sudden stop in traffic back in Boise. But as the cars slowly inched forward, we saw a giant elk grazing in the woods along the side of the road.

"Wow," Mike said. "Girls, look at the elk."

"Where?" said Emilia.

"I don't see it," said Ivy.

"Girls, there's a seven-hundred-pound animal standing ten feet away from our truck. How can you not see it?"

"I see it! I see it!" they chanted.

The line of cars moved an inch every minute as everyone ogled the massive creature.

"Don't do anything stupid, people," Mike muttered, with the other drivers in mind. "Don't honk, don't hog it, take your picture, and move along." He was agitated that the other drivers weren't more efficient when it was their turn closest to the animal, but he took his time when we had the prime viewing spot.

"What happened to 'take your picture and move along'?" I asked.

"It's just so cool," he answered. "I don't know if we'll see another one this close."

"It's a shame there isn't room to park," I said. With no safe area to stop along the narrow road and continue observing the animal, we reluctantly moved on, marveling at our luck.

After checking in to our cabin and a cursory glance at the grounds, we headed back to town to find a grocery store, to add something to our diet beyond hot-dog buns, tortilla chips, and beer. The elk *still* grazed at the side of the woods, only this time people parked their cars haphazardly half-on and half-off the road. Spectating caused a traffic jam with cars slowing as they passed, as before, while others walked around, as if to approach the animal. Some drivers honked, which didn't alarm the elk, while others belligerently blocked the road and took no heed of their fellow drivers. The small stretch of road became a gridlocked, chaotic mess.

"This is so stupid and wrong," Mike said.

"What is that woman doing?" A thirty-something held her toddler's hand and walked close to the elk.

"She's willfully taking her three-year-old within feet of a seven-hundred-pound wild animal," Mike answered.

"People are idiots."

"What did you say, Mom?" Ivy asked.

"I said that sometimes people don't make wise decisions."

Ivy whispered to her sister, "That's not what she said."

In truth, we encountered wonderful people in Canada, and as many Australians as Canadians, as every waiter or waitress we met greeted us with the telltale accent of the land Down Under. This was all that Emilia would need to launch an endless monologue detailing every day of our two months traveling throughout Australia. To turn the monologue into more of a dialogue, we encouraged Emilia to interview one of the waitresses at a pizza joint in Jasper. The interview began with, "I'm your host, Emilia, and welcome to 'Girl Around the World.' Tell me your name and where we are." Five minutes later, the same podcast ended with "That's it for 'Girl Around the World.' Thanks so much for joining me . . . uh . . . what was your name again?"

Before we moved on from the rented cabin at Patricia Lake Bungalows, we took advantage of what the property offered. This included renting a small boat to row around Patricia Lake.

"Be careful getting in," I warned as we awkwardly entered the boat. I am always sure that something will fall overboard—a cooler, a set of keys, a person. We managed to keep all of these in the boat, and Mike rowed us out into the middle of the lake.

"Is it my turn?" Ivy asked. "I want to row."

"Go for it," Mike said. "You row on one side, and Emilia can row the other."

"Ivy and I can be your boat drivers, and you and Mom can just relax," said Emilia.

"Sounds good to me," I said.

Twenty-five seconds later, Emilia's arms were tired, and Ivy needed a snack.

"I'll take a turn," I volunteered, and we made our way to the far side of the lake, where we drifted contentedly for a time before a bank of approaching dark clouds gave us good cause to head back.

We didn't know it at the time, but an interesting piece of World War II history lurked beneath us. With steel and aluminum in short supply, the British had embarked on a plan to build a floating island that would essentially be used as an aircraft carrier out of pykrete, a composite material of ice and wood pulp. Secret experiments to develop pykrete and test its strength, ensuring that it wouldn't shatter like pure ice, took place at a London meat market, in a meat locker behind a screen of frozen carcasses. Construction of a prototype of the vessel took place at Patricia Lake. Remnants of the prototype's wooden hull, ductwork, and insulation materials are still strewn along the bottom of the lake.

Ultimately, the plan to build an aircraft carrier from reinforced ice was abandoned, due to the impracticality of the costs involved. It turned out that the amount of steel needed for a refrigeration plant to freeze the pykrete was greater than the amount of steel needed for an aircraft carrier. Other critics argued that the amount of wood pulp needed for the pykrete was so great as to affect paper production. There's also the hitch of needing to maintain the material at or below freezing temperatures. The plus of having an aircraft carrier that won't sink is somewhat negated by the fact that it might melt.

"Maybe we can go in the hot tub," Emilia suggested as we walked up the steep path from the lake. At the top, we looked to see that the hot tub was vacant.

"Sure," agreed Mike. "It looks like a good time to go in."

We briefly returned to our cabin for towels and swimsuits. By the time we reached the hot tub, another family was using it. Thus began the awkward hemming and hawing as Mike and I muttered to each other about whether or not we should change the plan. I truly enjoy meeting other people during our travels, I just don't always want to do so while wearing a bathing suit and sharing a tub of warm water.

"Come on, guys," Emilia called loudly. "There's plenty of room." She and Ivy were already making friends.

"Yeah, I guess we're doing this."

Emilia chatted with our tub-mates, two girls with their mother and grandmother, with the ease of a cruise director while Ivy hovered at her side or smothered me in what I've come to think of as an endurance hug.

We capped off the day by roasting hot dogs and s'mores over a fire at one of the camp's large shelters. This stunning display of nutrition was accompanied by beer for Mike and wine for myself, and I resolved to add greater levels of exercise and vegetable consumption to my near future.

* * *

Don't Forget the Bear Spray

If it is a grizzly bear and it's going to make contact, drop to the ground and play dead and give the spray time to take effect. If it is a black bear, prepare to fight aggressively with any available weapons (fists, sticks, rocks, etc.) until the spray has time to take effect. Bear spray has been shown to reduce the length and severity of maulings.

—Center for Wildlife Information

On our last night in Jasper, we moved from Patricia Lake Bungalows to Jasper National Park, where we'd reserved an oTENTik, a cross between a cabin and a tent. The structures have log foundations but walls and roofs made of thick canvas. It took me only a week to realize that oTENTik was a camping play on the word authentic.

Campgrounds were a viable alternative to hotels for us, given that we had sleeping bags and other camping gear that we'd used at the cabin in Idaho. When we checked in to the Canadian campground, however, we were given more warnings than I'd anticipated.

"Don't keep just your food in your vehicle but also any deodorants and lotions," a ranger warned me. "We had a grizzly run through the campsite earlier today, so be very aware."

I wasn't sure how I felt about such information. I wanted to know the bear's backstory. Was it running from the scene of a crime? Or running after prey? Or just out for a jog? And what is the appropriate response if a grizzly runs by one's camp, other than pissing oneself? But we passed the evening in safety and without incident, save for the unfortunate overflowing of a commode at the nearest women's restroom. Karma, perhaps, for having wished a clogged toilet on the litterbug in Sandpoint. Other than that, the oTENTik experience was a positive one, and Mike and I woke at dawn the next morning.

"I'll start a fire," he whispered as we silently snuck outside, "and we can get some coffee going." A minute later, as we puttered around the fire, Mike said my name in a hushed voice. I thought it odd of him to continue whispering now that we were outside. Surely, we wouldn't wake the girls from such a distance. "Look." He pointed through the trees.

"Oh shit," I whisper-shouted back at him. "Is it a bear? Where's the bear spray?" I envisioned Mike handling the bear deterrent. This would be difficult, as we hadn't yet taken it out of the packaging, which looked like it would require bolt cutters to get through; nor had we practiced with the practice canister, ostensibly included so that if you needed to use the real bear spray, you could do so without accidentally pepper spraying yourself in the face. While Mike would tackle this task, I'd grab our kids and lock them in the truck, which would surely be safer than the oTENTik. Then I'd look for a pack of hot dogs to throw at the bear, hoping it would opt for processed meat logs over fresh human. But we no longer had a pack of hot dogs. I pictured the pack of breath mints on the dash and wondered if that would suffice.

"No, honey. Look. There are two elk," he said.

"Oh. That's really cool," I whispered back. "And maybe later today we should give that bear spray practice thing a try."

"Let's see if we can get a closer look," he said.

We crept through the woods but gave the animals their space and watched them graze in the silent morning.

"Is it weird that we're the only ones awake?" I asked.

"I know. I can't believe we're the only ones seeing this."

"Let's go back to the fire," I said. "I don't want to be too far away when the girls wake up."

Over the next thirty minutes, as we sipped coffee by the fire, we watched the elk come closer. Two elk turned to five, then eight. The highest we counted was twelve and two calves.

"Wow, they just keep getting closer," I said. They weren't interested in us or looking for food beyond the grass on which they grazed, but neither were they concerned by our presence or the fire.

We heard footsteps from inside the oTENTik, and Emilia and Ivy emerged, eyelids at half-mast.

"Girls, look around," Mike said.

"What?" Emilia asked. "The fire?"

Ivy yawned and crawled into my lap in one of our camping chairs.

"Look around," Mike repeated. Both girls did so.

"Oh! Gee!" said Ivy.

"Whoa," Emilia added. "Look at the size of these deer!"

"They're elk," Mike said. "And look over there. You'll see two babies."

"But we want to stay fairly quiet so that we don't scare

them away," I instructed.

"Somehow I don't think that's a concern anymore," Mike said.

Much of the camp was awake by this point. Many people had fires lit, and car doors occasionally slammed. The elk paid no attention.

"Now they're almost too close," I said. An elk grazed next to our car, another at the side of the oTENTik, unconcerned with being a mere fifteen feet from both humans and fire. In all, we watched them for about an hour before they collectively moved off through the woods.

Later that day, we left Jasper, headed for Prince George, and I realized why Canada seemed so pristine and beautiful to me. The breathtaking views and iridescent water were phenomenal, but just as important as what we saw was what we did not. There was a notable absence of litter, both in small towns and along endless stretches of highway. This was a contrast to what I'm used to, including routinely picking up trash discarded in my front yard.

"Is that a . . ." Mike interrupted my thoughts and slowed the truck to a stop along the side of the road. The opposite side of the road was flanked by a twenty-foot rock face, above which grew thick forest. At the edge of the forest stood a black bear.

"A bear!" both girls screamed.

"It looks like a big, cuddly dog," I said. Not that I had any intention of attempting to cuddle with it. But neither was I panicking and reaching for the bear spray, feeling no danger due to the distance and safety of our vehicle. Smokey Bear was a black bear. The teddy bear and Winnie the Pooh were inspired by black bears. I'm not above letting commercial caricatures of animals influence how I view them. At the same time, black bears are more than capable of mauling and killing a full-grown human, so cuddling was definitely out. We watched for a moment until the bear wandered off into the forest.

Prince George, the largest city in northern British Columbia, is a fairly industrial city of seventy-four thousand people at the confluence of the Nechako and Fraser Rivers. The industry, including an oil refinery, pulp mills, and sawmills, combined with the city's geography, which situates much of it in a valley, is an unfortunate recipe for significant air pollution. Deaths due to diseases associated with air pollution are reportedly higher in Prince George than in any other community in the BC province. The city also contends with the confluence of two major rivers in a low-lying area. The result is recurring flooding and, when temperatures drop, ice jams. In January 2008, an amphibious excavator and a system of piping in warm water were used to battle an ice jam that had grown to sixteen miles in length. If only they'd mixed in some wood pulp, they could have had an aircraft carrier.

We stopped for one night at a rented home outside of Prince George. As soon as we entered, I knew that the place was far too nice for our family of four, and I was glad we were only staying for one night. While others might prefer fine accommodations, I panic at the thought of what damage we might cause.

"Ooh, look. A piano!" Emilia said.

"Don't touch that," I barked.

"What's this?" Ivy asked.

"That's a cello," answered Mike. "And don't touch it."

"And they have a violin," Emilia said.

"How about you guys pick something to read from the bookshelf," I suggested. They settled on an old comic book and were content until I began to wonder if the comic was a priceless first edition of some kind. If the homeowners had comic books, chances are they were something special. We didn't linger at the home but stayed long enough to do a few loads of laundry, sorely needed after a week on the road and in various campsites, and to get a good night's sleep.

We continued our journey through the Bulkley-Nechako district, which included passing the Piper's Glen Resort that enticed weary travelers with the assertion, "It's Just Viewtiful!" Road signs along the way promised heavy moose populations, though we didn't catch sight of any of the giant creatures.

"Hey, Mom," Emilia said from the backseat, "I just had a thought."

"Okay."

"If I ever have two dollars, I mean two daughters, their names will be Caramel and Corlene."

"Oh. Okay."

"I just thought I'd let you know."

This is a good example of the level of conversation after a week in the car together.

"Does that say 'Overweight Foods'?" Mike asked.

I glanced at a grocery store we passed while driving through a small town. "It says 'Overwaitea Foods.'"

"That's not much better," Mike said.

"Right. You don't want people to have the word overweight in their minds when they're grocery shopping."

We had one more night to spend in Canada, another rented home in which to stock up on sleep before boarding the ferry for our day-and-a-half journey to Sitka. The townhome in Smithers, where residents often refer to themselves as Smithereens, had an incredible view of the Bulkley River, and I spent the evening glancing out the window hoping that a moose or a bear, or better yet a moose and a bear who were good friends and would frolic together for a bit for our enjoyment, would pass by. Sadly, this didn't happen.

The drive to Prince Rupert, the departure city for our ferry travel, is a unique one. The city is located on Kaien Island and linked to the mainland by a short bridge. After crossing the bridge, the Yellowhead Highway snakes along the water for a time before traveling through forested areas, eventually winding to the northwest corner of the island and the port city. When we arrived, Prince Rupert was gray and blanketed with steady, fine rain. It's known as "The City of Rainbows," which is a glass-is-half-full way of acknowledging Prince Rupert as Canada's wettest city, with over one hundred inches of annual precipitation and only twelve hundred hours of sunshine per year. But at least those twelve hundred hours include rainbows.

We checked in at the ferry terminal, where we learned that we should return by 12:45 a.m. for our 3:30 a.m. departure. With the rest of the day and half the night to kill, we occupied our time by cruising around town and stocking up on necessities. Parked outside of a liquor store (first things first), I opted to wait in the truck while Mike ran inside.

"Well, that was weird," he said when he returned. "They sell beer, but they don't sell *cold* beer. We have to go to a different store for that."

"If we must, we must."

And we did.

"Let's go check out that place," Mike said as we drove

along Second Avenue and parked in front of Slickers Raingear Warehouse. "It might be a good idea to get the girls some boots."

The purchase of Ivy's bright yellow boots and Emilia's purple boots may have been the most important of the entire trip. My daughters have been known to ruin a pair of sneakers simply retrieving the mail, and if the steady drizzle of Prince Rupert was any indication of the weather to come, the boots would prove invaluable.

"Maybe I should get some boots, too," I said.

"You can look, but they're kind of expensive." Mike already had a pair of Xtratufs, the preferred footwear of Southeast Alaska, but my boots were more fashionable and less sturdy. His comment about them being pricey kept me from looking, a decision I'd later regret when sprawled on slippery ground.

As we returned to the car, I studied the Moby Dick Inn across the street. A giant mural of a white whale breaching out of the sea decorated the side of the building.

"If we were staying overnight, you'd opt for the Moby Dick Inn, wouldn't you?" Mike asked.

"I can't help it," I conceded. "It just calls to me."

Long after dark, we parked in a line of cars at the ferry terminal. The children slept in the back while Mike and I attempted to stay awake, caught in the terrible cycle of drifting off until our heads bobbed forward, at which point we'd wake with a start and sit up straight, only to drift off again a moment later. The journey and long drives had taken their toll, and we were eager to reach Alaskan waters.

* * *

Matanuska

Alaska Marine Highway ships run for 8,834 miles from Bellingham north to Skagway, across the Gulf of Alaska, into Prince William Sound, and out to Dutch Harbor, the tip of the Aleutians.

—AlaskaTrekker.com

At four o'clock in the morning, we boarded the *MV Matanuska*. The 408-foot vessel was built in 1963 but lengthened and renovated in 1968, and it now accommodates up to eighty-eight vehicles and 499 passengers. All of which leads me to the question: How exactly does one *lengthen* a massive ferry?

We locked the car, loaded up with backpacks and a small cooler, and trudged wearily up to the purser's office to get the keys to our cabin. At some point while planning the trip, Mike had suggested the possibility of traveling *without* a cabin.

"It's a lot cheaper," he'd said. "Growing up, we used to do it all the time. We can take our sleeping bags up to the solarium. Lots of people do it. They pitch tents up there."

"Do you even know who I am?" I'd asked.

I can sleep in a tent. I can sleep on a boat. I can even, when a shortage of private accommodations and an abundance of hostel cots necessitate, sleep in cramped quarters and in close proximity to people who are not my immediate family. But the perfect storm of these conditions when there are other options? No way in hell.

Our cabin on the *Matanuska* was larger than any ferry cabin I'd seen and roughly twice the size of our four-berth cabin on the *Spirit of Tasmania* during our Australia trip. The *Matanuska* offered not only bigger berths and a larger bathroom but also a desk and table with area around it for arranging chairs.

"We could set up a little bar area in here," I said.

"Huh," said Mike. "I was thinking we could use the desk for, you know, work."

"Well, I guess you could. Is this much room normal?" I asked.

"No way," said Mike. "I didn't even know rooms like this existed."

"Look at the bunks. We could even . . . snuggle," I said.

"I want to snuggle!" Ivy proclaimed.

"I was talking about me and Dad."

"That's gross," Emilia declared.

"Oh. Then I want one of the top bunks," said Ivy.

"I'll take the other top bunk," Emilia suggested.

The girls quickly tucked in to the upper bunks while Mike and I nestled into a low bunk to get some rest. This lasted a full minute and a half before a desire for our own space won out over the inclination to share a bunk, and Mike moved to his own bed.

A few hours later, our window began to glow with a deep blue that brightened into sunshine as morning broke the night.

Mike stirred first, as he's apt to do. He wakes and rises, while I wake and think about rising for a good hour before attempting an upright posture. He crept to the window.

"Can you tell where we are?" I whispered. He was familiar enough with Southeast Alaska and the ferry system that he'd easily be able to identify our nearest city. This knowledge came not only from his Alaskan upbringing but also from a summer college internship aboard another of the Alaska Marine Highway's fleet, the *MV Kennicott*.

"Unfortunately, yes."

"What does that mean?"

"We're still in Prince Rupert."

"What? How long have we been on this ferry?"

"At least four hours. There must have been some sort of delay."

Despite the itinerary hitch, we later revisited the purser's office and learned that our estimated arrival time had not changed, and shortened stops in ports along our journey would put us back on schedule.

The *MV Matanuska* traveled along the Inside Passage, a network of waterways that weaves through the islands of northwest Washington, Canada, and Alaska. We'd stop in Ketchikan, Wrangell, and Petersburg before reaching our destination city of Sitka. Traveling the Inside Passage provides a buffer from more severe weather that vessels might experience on the open ocean, and the Passage isn't navigated only by ferries but also cruise ships, tugs, freighters, and fishing boats. It also provides access to remote villages dotting the coast, which can't be reached by roadways.

A good friend, and one of Mike's business partners in Boise, grew up in Gustavus, Alaska. While the "city" now enjoys a booming population of over four hundred, it was just over two hundred when Jared lived there.

"There were five people in my graduating class," Jared told me.

"Wow. I guess dating as a teenager must have been tough."

"There wasn't really dating. I had to go to junior prom with my cousin." He laughed.

"That sounds awful," I ventured.

"The socialization part of it was rough. I couldn't play football or baseball, and we could barely scrape together enough people for a basketball team. No movie theaters, no restaurants, and then in the winter you're talking about five hours of daylight, max. In the winter, there was just *nothing* to do."

"I bet people drank a lot," I said, thinking about how much alcohol I'd go through living in such a place.

"But it wasn't all bad," he said. "The outdoor aspects of it were amazing. Absolutely world-class sport fishing. And I mean, I could shoot a moose from my back porch if I wanted."

Apparently, to a teenage boy who grew up hunting, this sounds like a really delightful way to spend an afternoon.

"And I'd say we had a lot more freedom growing up than most kids," he continued. "There were no cops."

"Was there a hospital?"

He laughed again. "We had a clinic that was sort of like a little trailer. If it was a real emergency, you could drive to the airport and get someone to fly you to Juneau."

"I can't imagine the lack of anonymity. There's something comforting in being able to go somewhere that has no familiar faces."

"In the summer, the population could jump up by a

thousand people."

"Because of the fishing industry?" I asked.

"Because of Glacier Bay National Park. The tourists get there by cruise ship or fly into Gustavus."

In recent years, the Alaska Marine Highway added regular service from Juneau to Gustavus, which also facilitates tourism to the park. Would-be visitors to Glacier Bay National Park are cautioned about bringing their vehicles, however, as the park is almost entirely roadless, with most areas accessible only via foot, plane, or boat. The National Park Service website lists one "primitive campground," accessible only on foot.[2] I think of campgrounds as inherently primitive. The need to warn campers of a campground's primitive nature is a nice way of saying, "If you come here, you better have your shit together." Primitive as it is, the campground does include bear-proof food storage caches, and stays are limited to fourteen days. The presence of bear-proof food storage caches is enough to convince me that I'm not going to be spending two weeks camping there.

We spent much of our time on the *Matanuska* roaming around, and I was eager to see the solarium, the area in which Mike had suggested we set up camp to save money, where he'd spent many nights of his youth, often traveling with the Sitka High School wrestling team to compete with schools in other Alaskan cities. This was one of many differences in the experiences of our formative years. The act of leaving town, even for just a few hours for a sporting competition, necessitates travel by boat or plane for Southeast Alaskans.

But maybe the solarium wouldn't have been so bad. I wondered if I'd been too prissy and hasty in my dismissal of sleeping on the upper deck. Had I lost my sense of adventure?

Was this a marker of approaching middle age?

As we made our way to the upper deck, I contemplated what a terrible bore I'd become. There we found a roving pack of adolescent boys, a team of some sort, as evidenced by their matching maroon jerseys. Unsupervised, as far as we could tell, they climbed up a wall of lockers where passengers could secure their possessions, ran and screamed in blurs of young testosterone, and threw cups of water at one another. Had we opted to sleep in the solarium, these might have been our bunkmates, and I could think of few more uncomfortable situations than sleeping on the hard deck of a ship while sandwiched on all sides by wild, damp twelve-year-olds.

"Mom, what's that kid doing?" Emilia asked. She pointed to the wall of lockers, where the boys had transitioned from climbing the lockers to enclosing themselves *inside* the lockers. The metal cubes were just large enough for a boy to fold himself into a tight ball inside and then pull the door shut.

I'm no stranger to bad ideas. Throughout my life, I've put myself in unwise situations, conducted myself with despicable behavior, and embarrassed myself on levels that could rival even the greatest of jackasses on this planet. But willingly enclosing oneself in a metal box on a marine vessel has to be up there in the top-ten all-time worst ideas in the history of human thinking.

"That kid is doing something really stupid," Mike answered.

I looked around for an adult, or even an older teen, anyone in a matching maroon jersey who might be charged with the care of these minors. I saw no one and couldn't stay silent.

"Out of the lockers, boys," I boomed. "These aren't toys, and that's dangerous." Adults around me looked up from their novels and magazines and tablets. Most nodded slightly in agreement with my command, but I was shocked that no one else had felt compelled to speak. One by one, the boys emerged like ants fleeing a flooded nest, and I realized that while I'd thought half a dozen boys had shut themselves in lockers, the number was far greater.

Some of the boys walked away with heads hung with sullen, guilty looks, while others scowled directly at me, communicating their displeasure just short of muttering what a bitch I was. I wasn't fazed. I could imagine the headlines detailing the horrific and preventable deaths of two-dozen innocent youths, unable to reach life jackets and other safety measures during a maritime disaster because they were too busy pretending to be stowed backpacks. Mike smirked at me.

"What are you laughing at?" I asked.

"You just had to say something," he said.

"I'm not done yet."

We made yet another trip to the purser's office, where I informed the purser of the events taking place on the upper deck. She thanked me and made repeated (and unanswered) announcements calling for the guardian of the team to report to her. I pictured a coach somewhere on board, sneaking cans of Rainier and pretending not to hear.

Because of the space our cabin afforded us, we didn't have to spend all of our time roaming the ship and imposing my personal rules of conduct on young boys. We walked the ship, returned to the cabin for naps, games of Uno and Sleeping Queens, snacks, and beverages, and then walked the ship again.

One of the rooms held theater-style seating and small mounted screens at one end, on which were shown short films about Ketchikan, controversies in the fishing industry (*Friends don't let friends eat farmed fish!*), and Tlingit heritage, whose language and culture dies a steady death of white-imposed "civilization."

I worried my daughters' patience would wane with the serious subject matter and lack of animation, until Emilia commented on how cool it was to have free movies on board.

"But I'm still hungry," Ivy said, "and I'm tired of peanut butter and jelly sandwiches."

"Okay, how about ham and cheese?" I offered.

She rolled her eyes with force.

"I think maybe tonight we should spring for the cafeteria," Mike suggested. To save money, we'd been eating out of our cooler, but the repetitive diet grew tiresome.

"Okay," I agreed. "We should connect with Melissa anyway."

My longtime, seldom-seen friend Melissa deserved much of the credit for my present situation. I'd met her as a twenty-year-old exchange student in Moscow, Russia. (Sarah Palin likely watched our budding friendship from her backyard.) Originally from Sitka, Melissa graciously maintained our friendship after we left the motherland by inviting me to Sitka and later to Cabo San Lucas to celebrate Christmas with her family. The latter trip would be the love-at-almost-first-sight meeting with Mike that shaped our lives ever since.

Melissa had lived the previous decade in Boston after marrying her husband, Michael, who was ironically my husband's best friend growing up. They had two children of their own. Michael was already in Sitka with their kids, feeling his way around a new job, while Melissa, in the course of relocating their vehicle and remaining possessions from their life on the East Coast, coincidentally ended up on the same *Matanuska* ride as we did.

"Mom," Ivy whispered confidentially after we met Melissa in the cafeteria and settled at a table with our plates of food on plastic trays, "she looks like a princess." Melissa is gifted with a striking contrast of pale skin and dark features, and she's accustomed to moving about the world and encountering people who are overwhelmingly taken by her.

It was wonderful to see Melissa after so many years apart, but startling at the same time.

"I can't believe we're on the same ferry," she said.

"I can't believe you're moving back to Sitka," I added.

"I can't believe all four of us . . . well, eight of us when you count the kids, are all going to be in Sitka at the same time," Mike said.

The odds against such a confluence were great. When Melissa left Sitka after high school, she vowed never again to call Alaska home. Our own trips to Alaska averaged about one per decade, and with the advent of careers, kids, and life in general, the chances of our two families connecting had been slim.

"So, do you have kids?" Emilia asked.

"I do," Melissa answered with a smile. "I have a boy and a girl."

"Well, where are they? Can we play with them?"

"They're already in Sitka. You'll get plenty of time to play with them," Melissa assured her, "once we get there."

Emilia beamed, Ivy smiled shyly, and I made a mental note to let them know that this didn't mean Melissa's children would be waiting with toys at a welcoming playground when we docked in Sitka.

"Melissa," Ivy said, "you're very pretty."

Ivy is adept at the girl crush, as fascinated by beautiful women as by boys who pull her pigtails. This would seem to indicate a disproportionate emphasis on physical appearance, but while Ivy recognizes striking physical beauty like Melissa's, she's also apt to give the same compliment to the disfigured, acne-riddled, and overweight, as long as they have a genuine smile and something sparkly somewhere on their person.

"Thank you, Ivy," Melissa answered. "You're very pretty, too."

A second later, Emilia, gnawing on an overcooked rib, looked up at our group with a barbeque-sauced face and said, "Man, I just love eating meat off the bone."

Had she her way, Emilia would have had leftover ribs for breakfast the next morning, but we returned to the practice of preparing our grocery store goods in the ship's communal makeshift kitchen, resulting in bagels and cream cheese and instant coffee, all in an effort to reduce the expenses of our trip. Which isn't to say that we skimped entirely, as we had Baileys on hand to make the instant coffee taste less . . . instant.

After breakfast, as we cruised closer to Sitka, Mike spent more of his time glued to the vessel's windows, peering at the Alaskan islands and their coastlines through binoculars.

"What do you see?" I asked.

"Nothing yet," he answered, though he kept the binoculars pressed to his face.

"You really want to see a brown bear, don't you?"

"That would be cool," he confirmed. The black bear sighting had been memorable, but he really wanted to spot the larger, more aggressive brown bear.

"And if we're going to see a brown bear," I added, "I'd rather do so from a ferry boat than a bicycle." I was referencing Mike's most up-close encounter with Alaskan brown bears when, as a teenager, he rounded a mountain path and skidded to a halt in front of two large bears. One hunched on all fours while the other stood on hind legs. Mike froze and stared at the animals until he felt it safe to slowly backtrack. Having done so and removed himself from danger, he realized that his newly purchased twenty-dollar bike pump had fallen off at his encounter with the bears. With the wisdom of a seventeen-year-old, he willingly returned to the site to retrieve the bike pump. I've heard this story a dozen times in the course of our marriage, but my incredulity never wanes.

"So you went *back* for the twenty-dollar bike pump?" I ask.

"Well, it was brand new," he insists.

"And the bears were still there?"

"Yeah, they didn't like it when I came back," he says. "But like I said, I wanted to get my bike pump back. I couldn't just leave it there."

"Actually," I say, "I'm pretty sure you could have."

* * *

Island Life

Look at the slugs before you kill them. Say "poor slugs", and "I'm sorry, but I hope you taste yummy." Then pick off any large pieces of dirt. Drop slugs into a bowl with ½ vinegar, ½ hot water. Soak for 10 minutes or so to kill them and remove slime.

—Rickshaw Unschooling

With only fourteen miles of road from one end of Sitka to the other, there's no such thing as a long drive. This went a fair distance in helping me understand my husband's impatience with traffic and lines. He didn't grow up with such things, so when he encounters them in adult life, he becomes undone, irrationally panicking as if the earth has paused in its rotation and doom is imminent. Though he can't stand imposed delays and wait times, neither is he a hurried person, which also seems a mark of his Alaskan upbringing. Sitka moves at a thoughtful pace, and Mike embraced this as we drove from the ferry terminal through town, slowing to spy on his now dilapidated childhood home, remarking at the emergence of buildings that had sprouted since our last visit.

We drove to the marina at Crescent Harbor and located

the fifteen-foot whaler that came with a home we'd rented on nearby Bamdoroshni Island. I imagine there's considerable difficulty in renting out an island home if you don't also provide a means of getting there.

"Listen up, girls," Mike said. "This is very important. You need to wear your life jackets every time we get on the boat. Got it? *Every* time."

"We know, Dad," Emilia said. "But where are we going to sit?"

"Let's see. You two can sit right up front here on this bin." He directed the girls to perch on a large plastic tub, filled with more life jackets, near the bow of the boat but inside the protective windscreen.

With Mike and I occupying the captain and passenger seats, respectively, this left a small area between our seats and the engine to transport luggage.

"We're definitely going to have to take more than one trip," I noted.

"We can leave some things in the truck," Mike said. "Like the cooler. We'll just take what food we have left in smaller bags."

When we had what could fit loaded aboard the tiny vessel, Mike fired up the engine, backed out of the slip, and slowly made his way around the main dock, which required a bit of precision maneuvering through a narrow channel and under the walkway that led up to the parking lot. I studied him, wondering if I'd be able to replicate his actions. Mike and I have vastly different experiences when it comes to driving. He was raised with boats as a predominant means of transportation and eventually went on to obtain his captain's license. As a city girl with no such qualifications, the only instance in which I'm of any navigational use is when it comes to parallel parking a car.

In open water, Mike picked up speed, and the girls giggled at the sensation. I studied the islands around, looking for signs of life and landmarks in an attempt to orient myself.

"We have to slow down at this one spot," Mike said, easing up on the speed. "It gets shallow through here."

"Do you need to be looking at a map or something?" I asked.

"No," he said. "I looked at it the other day."

I considered the fact that all I have to do is blink and I've already forgotten where I'm headed.

The dock at Bamdoroshni Island is a good indication of the activity that takes place on it. A few small boats are tied up, and the stairs leading up from the dock pass by an old shed with two kayaks leaning against it.

"So this is our island?" Ivy asked, as if we'd purchased it.

"This is where we'll be staying," I confirmed. "Let's see if we can find the house."

Bamdoroshni has no roads or commerce. It is a small island with six residences. As such, we needed to find our rented home via a network of narrow wooden planks that served as walkways. Mike led the way, and the girls and I followed along on the slippery boards. They'd been covered in abrasive tread to provide traction, but much of this had worn away over time.

"This is like a magic forest," Emilia said.

"It's a rain forest," Mike said.

"Do you know where you're going?" I asked. This isn't a question I normally pose to my husband, but the narrow path branched off at times, and the density of the forest made it impossible to see what was ahead.

"Well, I thought so, but now I'm not sure. You stay here. Let me run back and check." He set his considerable bags down and backtracked. As soon as he was out of sight, I felt an uncomfortable sensation of being utterly dependent on another person for survival. I stood with my children, in a forest on an island accessed by a boat I didn't know how to drive, wondering what I would do if Mike didn't return. *This would be such a dumb way to die*, I thought, *lost on an island that isn't very big*. I knew bears often swam between islands in Southeast Alaska. How often did bears visit Bamdoroshni?

"Okay," Mike said as he returned. "We just needed to make one other turn." We backtracked, set out on the right path, and the dense forest gave way to a clearing where a modest home looked out over a rocky cove. Adjacent to the house were a woodshed and a large fire pit, surrounded by giant logs and makeshift benches.

"Ooh, can we have s'mores?" Ivy asked.

"One step at a time," I replied. "How about we check out the house?"

A kitchen, living room, and two bedrooms comprised the main floor, all of which centered around a wood stove. It was light and bright, with a hot tub on one side of the home and an incredible view of the water on the other side. Parts of the home were dated or unfinished but not as much as I'd anticipated. I could only imagine the difficulties in building and maintaining a home on a small island without roads or even sidewalks.

"I want this to be my room," Emilia called.

"Where are you?" I asked.

"Upstairs."

Mike and I found stairs leading to an upper loft. "Not a chance," Mike said. The most luxurious aspect of the home was its view, and the best view was from the upstairs bedroom.

"That's not fair," she asserted and spent the next ten minutes sulking about it.

"I know," I agreed. "It's so unfair that you get to go to Alaska and live on an island, and you don't get the adults' bedroom." In such situations, my patience can be limited.

"This bathroom is funny," Ivy called from the lower level.

I joined her in the lone full bath downstairs. The tub was short but deeper than usual, as if extra depth would compensate for the inability to extend one's legs. In time we'd realize the full quirks of the shower, which included two temperature choices that I came to think of as Holy Freezing and Burning My Flesh.

"And that is a big spider," Ivy added, pointing to a monstrous arachnid on the wall. I dispatched him, but he would be one of many.

Once we'd checked out the house, it was time to head back to the boat for a return trip to Sitka. Unencumbered by baggage on the trail to the dock, I was able to take in more of our surroundings. The thick rain forest included thousands of red huckleberries, salmonberries, and blueberries, which instantly brought to mind the idea of making jam. I'd never before made jam, no one in my family regularly consumed jam, and I hadn't the slightest idea how to go about such a task. As a result, the girls would do a fair amount of berry picking during our island stay, but this yielded no jams, jellies, or pies. The closest I got was at one point mashing them in a failed attempt at making a vodka mixer.

While boughs of berries hung from just above the ground

to high overhead, the trail itself was home to frequent slugs. Don't picture your innocuous little garden slugs. The Pacific banana slug is a monster, and it wasn't uncommon for us to find slugs six inches in length. The slugs of Bamdoroshni weren't yellow, as their name implied, but more often a mottled dark green and black, as if gearing up in camouflage.

"Maybe we should have slugs for dinner tonight," Mike suggested.

"Dad! We are not eating slugs!" Ivy yelled.

"You're joking, right?" Emilia asked.

"I don't know. These guys look pretty meaty," he answered. "They might be delicious."

"Look, that one's the size of a hot-dog bun." I stepped over a particularly large specimen.

Slugs can be eaten, though with berries aplenty and endless waters to fish, I couldn't imagine why anyone would go through the trouble to do so. Most resources available regarding the preparation of slugs are by people who've made it their mission to research and sample consumables in nature, in an effort to eat sustainably and free themselves from dependence on grocery stores. I have great admiration for such people but no hankering to be invited over for dinner. Some recipes call for sautéing the slugs, while others suggest breading and frying them. This is, of course, after killing, gutting, and desliming the creatures.

"How about we just go to the grocery store," Emilia suggested.

"Okay," Mike relented. "But we'll definitely try slugs sometime before we leave Alaska."

We walked on in silence, with 90 percent certainty that he was joking.

Walking across the island, getting back in the boat, driving back to Crescent Harbor, tying up the boat, going up the ramp (steep at low tide) to the parking lot, and getting back in the truck made me realize the full process of living island life. There would be no such thing as a quick trip to the store, and I gained an appreciation for the full-time island dwellers who call the islands of the Sitka Sound home.

We hit the grocery store and liquor store with a clear knowledge that every item purchased would have to be carted along to truck, marina, boat, dock, and again hiked across the island to reach our rented home. This is a good means of combatting impulse buys.

As we left Crescent Harbor for the second time that day, to transport more luggage and our few groceries, we saw a group of young boys standing atop the rocks at the break-water, screaming and pointing. Two large sea lions, jauntily chomping on fish, caused the excitement. They played with their food, flinging the fish in the air before retrieving them and crunching more. I'd never thought of sea lions as brutal until that moment. Later I'd notice papers posted on the marina message board warning of an aggressive sea lion in the area and urging people not to feed it. The animal in question, dubbed a "2,500 pound terrorist" by local media[3], had been bold enough to jump on people's boats or rush them at fish-cleaning stations. Like any situation requiring the bear spray, this was an encounter I hoped to avoid.

Back at the island, we explored the rocky cove that the home overlooked. We spent hours investigating at different times of day to find a variety of creatures, depending on the tide. At low tide, walking along the rocky beach brought a crunching from underfoot as we crossed over barnacles and tiny mussels, intertwined with seaweed and teeming with life from millions of small crabs and snails. I voiced a small "I'm really sorry about this" with every step.

"Look at this one," Emilia said, holding up a miniscule but intact shell of a former crab.

"Yeah, that's neat," I said.

"I'm going to keep it."

"Well, you can't take it inside," I said.

"I can't?"

"No, we don't want the crab shells to stink."

"Oh." She looked thoughtful for a moment, then added, "Well, I guess I better get rid of these then." She dropped the shell and put both hands into her pockets, pulling out dozens of crab fragments.

At high tide, the cove presented a unique opportunity to paddle around the protected waters. We had both the inflatable stand-up paddleboard and an inflatable raft. But these were heavy items stowed in the bed of the truck, and the thought of trekking them across the island gave both Mike and me back spasms.

"I think I have a way around it," Mike said.

"Around what?"

"Around the island. We'll load the raft and paddleboard on the boat but bring it around to the cove at high tide instead of going to the dock."

"Is that safe?"

"Sure. I think I can do it."

"Your confidence is really reassuring."

"I think we should do it. The weather isn't always nice in Sitka, and the forecast is good for the next few days. It'd be a shame not to have the paddleboard here."

Thus we made yet another trip to Crescent Harbor and loaded the raft and paddleboard onto the boat. The girls took their usual posts at the helm, waving to other passing boats and to a couple sitting on the porch of a yellow home with a big greenhouse adjacent on another island. Mike expertly maneuvered the boat to the cove and somehow managed to unload the raft and paddleboard without the girls and me drifting out to sea.

"I can't believe you pulled that off," I said as he picked up speed to take the boat back around to the island's dock.

"You were freaking out, weren't you?"

"Yes, but I was at least trying to do so silently."

"Thanks for that."

The girls had their backs to us, and so, for a brief moment, I pulled my neckline down and flashed a boob at my husband. It's my secret means of saying "I love you" when no one is looking and a simultaneous attempt to be cooler than my inner turmoil, to counter my often uptight and nervous demeanor. Mike smiled at me in thanks, and I looked beyond him to see the yellow home we'd passed earlier, where the couple still sat, looking at us with open mouths.

* * *

Zarina

There's nothing—absolutely nothing—half so much worth doing as messing about in boats.

—Kenneth Grahame, *The Wind in the Willows*

As a child, I regretted that the bald eagle was the national bird of the United States. I'm sure such an admission will garner me labels of "un-American," but that's just how I felt. On the presidential seal and federal agency logos, the bird looks angry, downright pissed off. Sure, it's holding an olive branch—but also thirteen arrows. This symbolizes that we desire peace but are always ready for war, which to me says that we're not terribly optimistic about our prospects for peace.

Beyond that, the eagle's legs are spread wide. It's basically manspreading. It could have been designed as regally perched on a branch or a profile of it soaring through the air, but no, it has to splay its crotch to the world, which only makes me think of politicians who feel compelled to text pictures of their genitalia. It took six years and three committees to develop the seal, and no one thought to say, "Is it weird that the bird's legs are spread so wide?" Benjamin Franklin didn't support the selection of the bald eagle as the national bird, declaring it "a bird of bad moral character,"[4] though this had nothing to do with the crotch-splaying and stemmed more from the bird's predatory and opportunistic nature.

Though I still think we could have come up with a better representation of the bird for our coat of arms, I've since developed an appreciation for the bald eagle. They're impressive raptors and abundant in Southeast Alaska, having recovered from the days when it was popular to shoot the birds, as they were demonized and thought to be capable of carrying off lambs and small children. The other big threat to the birds was the use of the pesticide DDT. It's since been banned in the United States and Canada, but during DDT's heyday, its environmental impact caused sterility in birds or lessened their ability to produce healthy eggs. Females would lay eggs with brittle shells, and the weight of an adult eagle brooding over its egg would sadly crush it long before there was any chance of hatching. This is one of many instances of humans doing something that results in a really shitty outcome for nature.

The current healthy bald eagle population in Sitka resulted in up to fifty eagle sightings in any one day during our trip. We'd learn to look for the white head of an adult eagle against the green background of the treetops and could spot as well the mottled brown and white of adolescent birds.

Wildlife sightings in Southeast Alaska are plentiful but even more so when traveling by boat and increasing the amount of territory to observe. Such an opportunity presented itself to us when Melissa's parents invited us on their boat for an evening dinner cruise. The *Zarina* is home to Karen and Charlie for the summer months, while they spend their winters in Mexico. The differences in these two homes are vast, not only in climate, as Sitka is an exercise in how to live damply while the Mexican desert proves that turning human skin into leather is easier than one might think, but also as far as their actual residences. Charlie and Karen's life on the *Zarina* takes place in square footage equivalent to the kitchen of their spacious home in Mexico. The fact that they move seamlessly between these two contrasting homes and environments is a testament to their strength, adaptability, and continual sense of adventure.

When Mike and I were young, childless, and ramen-noodle poor, we had the chance to move onto a boat, to become live-aboards. The rent to live on the boat was half what we'd been paying for an apartment, so we lunged for the opportunity with optimism and naiveté.

The boat wasn't functional as a watercraft, just a floating place to live. I didn't mind having a marina for a neighborhood; the creaking of docks and the bells of buoys were almost soothing. The lack of running water, however, was a little more problematic. A middle-of-the-night pee meant either a bucket or a trek to the marina facilities. Cooking on a camping stove seemed quaint until it came time to wash dishes. When the rainy season came, we'd wake to find leaks in our bunk, and when the bilge pump stopped working, we'd step out of bed in the morning to find two inches of water on the floor. Needless to say, it quickly became difficult to romanticize life on the tiny Chris-Craft. We lasted three months.

Charlie and Karen's vessel, by contrast, was more than functional. The boat was a tri-cabin trawler, a forty-foot, fiberglass, 1978 DeFever and home to not only Karen and Charlie but also their two small dogs, Rosita and Chili. I wondered if Mike and the girls and I could live in such a small space. I thought the end result of such an experiment would be a cross between *The Swiss Family Robinson*, *Lord of the Flies*, and *The Shining*, so perhaps not a great idea.

In its original state, the *Zarina* would have brought to mind an old-style pleasure boat, but Charlie is a retired Alaskan commercial fisherman and as such geared up the boat with a washdown hose, Tufflex nonskid deck covering, and hydraulics for hauling in shrimp pots. Being invited to dinner by him and his wife is a dream for seafood whores like myself. In addition to the pleasures of their food and company, it's lovely to be invited out onto a boat. I think of boats in the same vein as swimming pools. I don't want to own one, because of the money and maintenance such things require. I just want to have friends who do.

Our dinner cruise was nearly cancelled when Charlie spent a day dismantling one of the *Zarina's* two toilets. "Boat heads" are notoriously finicky, whereas children are less discerning when it comes to what they'll place into a toilet bowl. Charlie and Karen's grandchildren had long since learned the severity of the reprimand they'd receive if toys or even toilet paper worked their way into the boat's toilets when they visited. And all grandchildren pleaded ignorance as to what could have caused the toilet in question to stop working. One of their granddaughters, however, had recently consumed a bowl of cherries along with two cherry pits, which, when passed through her system, were all that was necessary to wreak havoc on the *boat's* system. Luckily for us, but perhaps unfortunately for Charlie, he's adept at dismantling and reassembling a boat commode and was able to set it right again in time for our dinner cruise.

We met Karen and Charlie on the *Zarina* at their slip in Sealing Cove. After reviewing the rules with our children, including the necessity of wearing a life jacket when on the outer deck and remaining visible to the adults, as well as that there would be no such thing as privacy if they needed to use the facilities, to ensure we weren't the cause of any future toilet dismantling, we set out for Silver Bay.

"Is this pretty much top speed?" Mike asked as we puttered slowly through the water.

"This is about as fast as she goes," Charlie confirmed. "You're not going to get anywhere in a hurry." This was as it should be. If your mode of transportation is also your home, slow and careful makes sense. Both turtles and snails are clear confirmation of this.

Silver Bay, the deep-water fjord just southeast of town, is a picturesque, quiet spot to spend an evening on the water. Karen and Charlie offered gin and tonics, Moscow mules, and a dinner of shrimp, salmon, corn on the cob, and salad, all expertly produced from what nonboat people call a "teeny-tiny kitchen" but what boat people refer to as a "well-appointed galley."

"Dinner is fantastic," said Mike.

"I love salmon," said Emilia. "And shrimp. Not so much on the salad, though."

"Stop talking after you mention the things you like," Mike muttered.

"Yes, that was an excellent meal," I agreed.

"We should come back to your boat and do this again," Emilia insisted.

I try to keep her from inviting herself places, but in this case she was only voicing what the rest of us also wanted.

"Well, we hope you'll come back," Charlie said.

"Next time you come, we'll take the boat out even farther, and you can stay overnight," Karen suggested.

"Can we sleep down there?" Ivy asked with hopeful eyes, pointing to the second bedroom below. It had the appeal of a tree fort and the allure of a beckoning cave.

"You sure can," Karen confirmed. "And do you know where your mom and dad will sleep?"

I leaned forward, because if we were to do an overnight trip on the *Zarina*, I had no idea where Mike and I would fit in such plans.

"Right here," said Charlie, gesturing to the table around which we crowded.

"I don't think my mom is going to want to sleep on the dinner table," Ivy said.

"Don't worry," Charlie assured us. "It folds down into a bed."

"Like a Transformer," said Emilia.

I've been on enough boats and in plenty of campers to know this is true, that one piece of furniture can turn into another, that a dining table can quickly change into an adequate bed, but that knowledge couldn't keep the image from my mind of Mike and me curled awkwardly on the table as it was before us, attempting to keep limbs tucked in tight to avoid toppling onto the floor.

"There's something in the water over there that I want to check out," said Charlie after dinner.

Such statements get me very excited. Because whenever I think I see something interesting, an object I'm sure will turn out to be a rare animal sighting or lost treasure, it turns out to be a log. Or imaginary. But when a seasoned fisherman who's spent decades of his life on the water wants to check something out, it's probably going to be both real and more interesting than a log.

"It looks like a sea lion," said Karen.

"A dead one," added Charlie.

"How did it die?" Emilia asked as Charlie piloted the *Zarina* around the bloated animal. Its head and tail were submerged, but the sea lion's midsection hovered above the surface like a giant gray bubble rising from the water.

"I'm not sure," he answered.

"He hasn't exploded yet, but he will soon," said Karen. "That will make the seagulls happy."

I wasn't sure what to think. I know that the build up of gases during decomposition can cause a carcass to explode, but I didn't know with what level of intensity such an event would occur. Would it be on par with the lighting of a match head or a full-scale bomb? Was our proximity to the animal dangerous? Were we in the line of fire for potential sea lion shrapnel? Alaska is home to Steller sea lions. These are the twenty-five-hundred-pound variety, not the cute little California sort that balance beach balls on their noses at aquariums. If the deceased beast were to blow, would pounds of rotting sea lion flesh rain down upon us? As the only adult on board who hadn't lived in Alaska, I kept these questions to myself.

This prospect of an exploding animal was both gruesome and intriguing, and one of many things that Alaskans might have previously encountered but which seemed entirely alien to me. Mike grew up with experiences that included his father chaining fish carcasses to giant logs so that the family could observe bald eagles feeding on the remains. This has been described to me many times with nostalgia, as if all families engage in the activity. Like family game night, only different. Whenever I think of such stories as gruesome or odd, I remember that much of the communication between my mother and me centers on serial killers and unsolved crimes, and suddenly the barbaric nature of wild animals is downright wholesome in comparison. Nonetheless, as the *Zarina* eased its way back to Sealing Cove and away from the sea lion, I was glad we weren't there to watch it explode.

* * *

Fish Slayer

*Fishing is boring, unless you catch an actual fish,
and then it is disgusting.*

—Dave Barry

With a fifteen-foot whaler at our disposal, as well as tips on where to fish from seasoned mariners like Charlie, we decided to try our hand at fishing. For someone who can be squeamish about preparing and consuming meat, I'm surprisingly game for dealing with fish, scales and guts included.

The four of us crammed into the tiny boat with two rods, a newly purchased pack of hooks, fishing license, and semi-frozen herring and squid for bait.

"Maybe we'll get a few rockfish," Mike said.

"But is it possible we could get a halibut?" I asked.

"It's possible."

I had dreams of returning to landlocked Idaho with a fish box full of seafood. As soon as I dropped my hook in the water, I was sure I'd awaken my inner fisherman. Or fisherwoman.

I probably had an untapped knack for calling forth the sea's bounty. Local media would want to interview me. I'd harvest not just halibut but salmon, tuna, scallops, crab, and shrimp. Scallops in the Sitka Sound are a thing of the past and require diving gear, nor did we have crab or shrimp pots at our disposal, but a girl can dream.

We bobbed in between the islands dotting Southeast Alaskan waters, giving the girls turns at reeling in the line. This yielded nothing on our first few attempts, though every time the hook snagged the bottom or a giant growth of kelp, I was sure we'd instead hooked the mother lode and would be stocked with halibut for the foreseeable future.

"Dad, I think we got something," said Emilia as she reeled in a line.

"It's probably just more seaweed," Ivy guessed.

"Nope, that's a rockfish," Mike confirmed.

"Do we have a plan?" I asked excitedly. "Do we have a gaff hook or something to bring it in? And where are we going to put it?"

We looked at each other and realized we hadn't prepared for what to do if we actually caught something.

"Well, no real plan," he said. "But I do have a pair of pliers and a hammer."

While I'm sure this might horrify avid fishermen who pride themselves on their fishing accoutrements, we somehow made do with the pliers, hammer, and a plastic bag that the bait had come in. Mike pinned the fish to the deck under his Xtratufs, knocked it in the head with the hammer, then used the pliers to hold the fish by the mouth while removing the hook and uneaten bait, careful to avoid the fish's sharp spines.

"That is one ugly fish," said Emilia.

"But I bet it tastes good," I ventured.

"Let's do it again," said Ivy. "It's my turn this time."

"Why don't you take the captain's chair," Mike suggested. I did so as he helped the girls prepare the fishing rods for another go.

"Ooh, the captain's chair is comfy," I remarked. I mimed driving the boat, like an excited child permitted to sit behind a steering wheel for the first time.

"Take the boat back to where we were," he instructed. "We've drifted a bit."

"Wait, you want me to actually do something? The number of assumptions you just made is startling."

"What do you mean?"

I looked around at the water and surrounding islands. "I have no idea where we were, are, or need to be."

"Just look on here," he said, handing me his phone with an open app that showed sophisticated mapping software, or what I liked to think of as random dots and lines moving about on a tiny screen.

"This makes about as much sense to me as fantasy football."

"Just start heading north."

"You know I don't speak compass. I only understand right, left, straight, and backward."

"Okay, you see that island?" He pointed, and I nodded. "Go that way."

I turned the wheel. Nothing happened. The throttle sat to my right, but I was afraid to touch it. "See, this is another assumption. You think I actually know how to operate a boat."

The depth of Mike's patience matched the waters in which we drifted, and he took time to walk me through the basics of maneuvering the boat back to the ideal fishing spot. After twenty minutes as surrogate captain, I began to relish the role and reached a tentative comfort with the responsibility, given that there was nothing close enough for me to crash into. When the girls were both satisfied that they'd had a true fishing experience and we had three rockfish in the bag, we headed back to Bamdoroshni Island.

"Mom, when we get back to the house, can I have ramen?" Emilia asked.

"No," said Mike. "We did not just go fishing so that you can eat ramen noodles."

"Do you remember how to clean a fish?" I asked Mike. I had no problem doing so but also no idea how to begin.

"Yes," he said, but with a definite lack of confidence in his voice.

We reached the dock, tied up the boat, and hauled the remaining bait and the bag of our catch back across the island to the house.

"Are we going to cut the fish open now?" Ivy asked.

"Are we going to eat them?" added Emilia.

"I think so," I said, putting the bait back in the freezer for another day.

"Maybe we should watch some YouTube videos first," said Mike.

We spent the next twenty minutes watching online tutorials on cleaning and cooking rockfish. Many of the videos contradicted one another, so we decided to glean the most useful knowledge from each and combine them to form our own process. The first step was locating a large plastic cutting board so that we might keep the blood, scales, and other carnage to a minimum. Next we located a knife. The importance of a very sharp knife when fileting fish cannot be underestimated. The knives at our disposal were as sharp as plastic spoons.

"I think I got this," Mike said. He wore heavy rubber gloves to protect himself from the fish's spines and did a fair job fileting one half of a fish. Emilia and Ivy perched on the other side of the kitchen counter, watching with interest.

"Yeah, it looks like you're doing really good," I agreed.

Mike was about to flip the carcass to filet the other side when the fish came to life, flew violently into the air, and flopped on the kitchen floor.

"How can it still be alive?" Emilia shrieked. "You cut off half of its body!"

"I wonder if that's supposed to happen," said Ivy.

"Didn't you kill it first?" I asked.

"Of course I did. It's just a little residual twitching," Mike said.

"Residual twitching? It jumped three feet into the air!"

"Everyone, stay calm." He glared at me, willing me to calm down so that I didn't further alarm the kids.

"Right," I said. "Perfectly normal." Mike retrieved the possibly dead half of a rockfish from the floor and rinsed it off while I did my best to contain the spread of gore that was quickly taking over the kitchen. I'd find dried scales for weeks to come.

After Mike finished fileting the fish, I cleaned and trimmed the filets for cooking. Preparing fish often involves deworming them, which isn't something that seafood fanatics like myself like to think about, but it's true nonetheless. I first learned about worms in fish when I was in college and had a brief stint as a waitress at a sushi restaurant.

"What do you mean fish have worms?" I asked my roommate, who happened to be a sushi chef at the restaurant where I waited tables.

"It's true," she said. "One of the first things we do is pull out the worms."

I struggled with this knowledge. Worms were meant to be in dirt and occasionally in the digestive tracts of dogs. Not in fish. On the other hand, people used worms as bait. Maybe this was payback for plucking happy little earthworms from the ground, spearing them with hooks, submerging them in water, and feeding them to fish. I mean, that's a pretty shitty day, when you think about it. Maybe the tiny worms embedded in fish flesh were humans getting their just desserts. If you can consider worm-infested fish flesh a dessert.

I was further confronted with this reality when examining the rockfish in front of me. A single, tiny pink coil nestled in the white flesh of the fish. It was easily removed, and I vowed not to think about it again. Nor would I think about how many worms I'd probably consumed in my life.

Tuna sandwiches, fish sticks, fish and chips.

Nope.

I wouldn't think about it.

We froze the carcass in a plastic bag until we could take it to town later for disposal and set about cooking our catch.

"Do you want me to do it?" Mike asked.

"No, I'll give it a shot." I used flour, a beaten egg, and panko breading and fried up small strips of rockfish. "Let's try it, girls. I bet it's going to be great! Here, Ivy, take a bite." I held a forkful of fried fish up to her, and she winced slightly. "Come on, Ivy. It's just like fish and chips." Ivy is the more adventurous eater between her and her sister, and I was surprised that she balked for a moment.

"Okay," she said. I could tell that she didn't want to take a bite but was feeling pressured into it. The look of disgust on her face a moment later made me worry that perhaps what I'd created wasn't "just like fish and chips."

I took a bite myself and accepted the full failure of what I'd done. Forcing a kid to eat something before the parent has sampled it is a rookie move and one I've made before. I should have known better.

"Here, Ivy," I said, offering her a napkin. "Spit it out. I'm sorry I made you try that."

"Not good?" Mike asked.

"It's awful," I admitted. "Just bland and awful. And it definitely needs salt."

"Well, don't cook any more of it," Mike reprimanded. The implication was clear. I had no business ruining what we'd gone through so much to procure. "I want to try cooking the next batch myself."

"Go for it," I said. There was no point in trying to defend my culinary catastrophe. It was that bad.

Ivy enjoyed a winning streak of Uno against Emilia and me until Mike announced that dinner was ready.

"Are you going to make me eat the awful fish again?" Ivy asked.

"No, Ivy. This time it will be great," I assured her. "I'd never cooked fish like this before, so I just didn't do it right. But Dad grew up in Alaska, so I'm sure this time it will be delicious."

Mike placed a plate of fried fish in the middle of the table, along with tortillas and a few condiments. "Fish tacos!" he announced proudly.

We sat down to eat, the kids warily so. I made my taco and was the first to take a bite.

"How is it?" Mike asked.

"Um, it's a little bit salty," I answered.

It tasted like a salt taco. There's a reason why a salt taco isn't actually a thing.

"Oh," he said, after trying a bite of his own. "I guess I maybe went a little too far with the seasoning."

"Mom, do we have to eat this?" Emilia asked. Ivy looked about to cry.

"No, no you don't," I said. "Let me go see if we have any ramen."

* * *

With such unique accommodations as the island home, and in Sitka where we had many friends, we naturally wanted to host a few dinner parties during our stay. The guest list included Michael and Melissa, Charlie and Karen, and their daughter-in-law, Ashley, who lived on the island with her two small children while Dylan, Charlie and Karen's son, was out to sea fishing. The menu never included rockfish.

The dinner parties were a huge success when the weather was nice. The kids played together on the rocks of the small cove, we sat around bonfires and roasted marshmallows, and we enjoyed the incredible view from the deck. When the weather was less cooperative, dinner parties turned into fifteen people, a third of them small children, crammed together in a very small space.

"I have to make sure I can find my shoes later," Mike said in passing at one such gathering. I watched then as he shadowed three-year-old Lola, Ashley's daughter and a spitfire who had a penchant for relocating found shoes.

"At least she has clothes on," said Ashley. "That girl just wants to be naked all the time."

"I'm sure the shoes won't disappear," I called to Mike. "Come have a beer."

He did so and then helped me refill drinks for our guests. Melissa and Michael, along with their two children, brought Transformers for each of the other kids as gifts, but Lola seemed uninterested, while Emilia and Ivy were engrossed in the intricacies of theirs. I'd just topped off Ashley's drink and was secretly wondering when I'd get a chance to play with one of the Transformers when Ashley shouted, "Lola, no!" We all turned to see Lola crossing the living room with Mike's laptop held high overhead.

"Oh, god," Mike whispered. He is incredibly dependent on technology. His laptop and the work for which he uses it are what make our long-term travels possible. Seeing his laptop in danger fills him with panic and dread, the same anxieties I experience when running low on wine. But Ashley expertly retrieved the laptop and handed it to Mike. He turned to Lola then and asked, "Do you want to hide more of my shoes? You can have *all* of them."

* * *

Magic Island

It's odd the things that people remember. Parents will arrange a birthday party, certain it will stick in your mind forever. You'll have a nice time, then two years later you'll be like, "There was a pony there? Really? And a clown with one leg?"

—David Sedaris

"I'm pretty sure you're actually Wonder Woman," I said to Ashley as we stopped to chat in passing at the dock on Bamdoroshni.

"The long stretches of single parenting while Dylan's out fishing can be tough, but I manage." Her arms were laden with grocery bags, and her children buzzed in a whirlwind around her legs. "I'm glad I ran into you. Do you guys want to come to Jack's birthday party? It's tomorrow on Magic Island." Ashley and Dylan's firstborn, Jack, is older brother to three-year-old, shoe-snatching, laptop-wielding Lola.

"Tomorrow?" I asked.

"Yeah. All my friends are whining about the short notice, but I wanted to wait for Dylan, and I just found out he comes in tonight. Fishermen don't exactly get to set their schedules, and Jack didn't want to have his party without his dad there."

"Of course," I said. "We'd love to come."

"How old is Jack going to be?" Emilia asked.

"He'll be five," Ashley answered.

"I'm five!" Jack roared.

"Oh. I'm nine."

"Will there be cake?" Ivy asked.

"Yes," Ashley confirmed. "Cake and pizza and Nerf guns. Lola, honey, please keep your shirt on. I'd better go, but we'll see you guys tomorrow."

The next day, we traveled to town with the intent of stopping to buy a birthday gift before going to the party.

"What if we got him a kid's version of a tool belt or something like that?" I suggested.

"Or maybe magic tricks," said Emilia.

"Are you just saying that because you like magic tricks?" I challenged.

"Maybe," she confessed. "Are you suggesting a tool belt because you secretly want one?"

"No!" I insisted, while realizing that I had always secretly wanted a tool belt. I was sure wearing one would instantly make me handy. I'd measure things and fix things and get to write on walls with oddly large pencils.

Mike pulled into the parking lot of a True Value hardware store. We didn't buy any tool belts (for Jack or me), but as we walked deeper into the hardware store, which seemed without end, it morphed into something resembling a small department store, in the upstairs of which was a toy section.

"We should maybe get him this," Ivy said, holding up a toy shopping cart filled with plastic replicas of cupcakes and cookies.

"I'm just not sure that's a good fit for Jack," I said.

"I found this really cool set of books," Emilia offered. "And they're about trucks and things, so they'd be perfect for Jack because he's a boy, and boys like trucks."

"Those are chapter books, Emilia. I don't think he's quite ready for those."

"How about a rocket?" Mike asked.

We went with Mike's suggestion, a simple stomp rocket that didn't include anything with which Jack could hurt himself, unless you considered the harm he might cause himself with the tantrum that would occur when the rocket was inevitably stomped into an irretrievable state.

"Is this it for you?" the checker asked as I placed the rocket on the counter.

"Yes," I confirmed. "We're headed to a five-year-old's birthday party."

"Let me guess. Jack?"

"Yes!"

"He must be a popular little boy," she said. "Because I sure have had a lot of people in here buying presents for Jack." The short notice of the party, combined with a limited number of places in Sitka where one could buy a suitable present for a five-year-old, had caused a minor boom in business for True Value.

When I'd first heard of the party's location, I'd wondered what was so magical about Magic Island. We drove to a recreation area on Sitka's shore, where Ashley had claimed a picnic table and stacked it with pizza boxes. Parents chatted in small groups while twenty children ran around screaming (in delight, not terror) and playing tag. Magic Island was just offshore. Did someone have a skiff to shuttle us over? Were we to swim there? How had Ashley failed to mention such an important detail?

"Lola, no!" Ashley yelled. "Not yet!" I looked to see Lola at the water's edge, ready to trudge through the water to get to Magic Island.

My questions were answered when the tide receded, revealing a stretch of sand connecting to the island. The party had been timed for this. The children ate pizza and played while Ashley snuck over to the island to hide a treasure box. She returned and gathered the kids together just as a couple with two dogs crossed the stretch of sand for a stroll on the island.

"Okay, everyone," Ashley addressed the kids, ranging in age from three to ten. "Here's how it works. When I say go, you're going to go to Magic Island and search for the treasure box. Everybody ready? Go!"

Chaos ensued. The horde of children let out a battle cry and charged for the island. The couple out for a romantic walk turned to see the kids racing their way and surely felt under attack. Emilia joined the fray, while Ivy simply dropped her hands to her sides and began to cry, intimidated by the unfamiliar faces, territory, and frenzy.

"You don't have to go, Ivy," Mike said.

He comforted her while I chatted with Dylan. A longtime friend of ours, we'd first known Dylan as Charlie and Karen's son and Melissa's brother.

"It's so good to see you," I said. "How long are you in town?"

"We leave tonight," he answered. "I'm so tired."

"Wow, that's a quick turnaround."

I thought it must be hard to be a commercial fisherman.

It's hard work to begin with, but there's the added element of being away from your family. This made it difficult for Ashley, too, having to single-parent during Dylan's absences on an island, where every playdate or trip to the store or activity involved driving a boat into town. At the same time, I recognized that Dylan was born to fish. He was the son of a fisherman, grew up fishing, and was better at it than most. He'd spent his youth struggling in school, and I couldn't imagine forcing the kid version of Dylan to sit at a desk and endure traditional schooling. He is a born outdoorsman.

We caught up on each other's lives as the army of kids, now armed with the Nerf guns they'd found in the treasure box, returned to the picnic table area and battled it out around us. This is the type of situation in which I try to carry on a rational adult conversation while also suppressing the constant urge to flinch. Finding myself in the middle of a Nerf war is my personal version of hell, along with chewing gum in my hair, Chuck E. Cheese, and the fear of pooping in my sleep. Knowing that a Nerf bullet won't injure me does nothing to stifle the certain fear that I'm about to be hit.

"I think your party is a success," I said to Ashley as the warfare died down. "But I can't believe Dylan's leaving so soon."

"I know. It sucks. That's why the party had to be now."

"Good thinking."

"I heard tomorrow is supposed to be really sunny and warm, and those are rare days here. I was thinking we could have a little get-together on the island, invite some of the other moms out, have some champagne. What do you think?"

"Yes, please."

The next day was beautiful. The sun shone on the

protected cove behind our home, and the temperature was warm enough that the girls put on their bathing suits.

"I think we're going to have to break out the sunscreen," I said to Mike.

"I know. So awesome!"

"This doesn't feel like Alaska."

"Well, don't get used to it," he warned. "It could be followed by three weeks of rain."

The weather report did forecast interminable rain in the week to come, but I decided to pretend I hadn't seen it.

Ashley arrived with Jack and Lola, along with some of her friends and their children. Charlie brought Michael and Melissa's two children, and we all gathered our collective rafts and paddleboards. Once we life-jacketed the children, they were free to paddle about in the cove. Giant rocks jutting up at low tide became pirate islands, and brilliant orange and purple sea stars were alternately referred to as doubloons, treasure, and booty, the last of which prompted giggling. The adults set up a row of camping chairs from which we watched the children while sipping champagne and snacking on appetizers. I wavered between relaxing one minute with drink in hand and panicking the next as barefoot children navigated rocks by turns slippery and barnacle-covered.

"You must love living on the island," I said to Ashley. "I mean, I think to live like this permanently, you really *have* to love it."

"Yes," she confirmed. "You can't really go into this kind of thing half-assed. I do love it, and it's magical and it's amazing for Jack and Lola to be able to grow up on an island. But I'm not going to lie, sometimes it sucks. Last week Jack was playing with the hose outside, and he left it on, so then we were out of water for three days until it rained again."

"Ugh, so what do you do?"

"I have family in town, so I can always go in and stay with them, which is usually what I do when we're out of water. And the winter can be awful when there's ice on the dock and all the lines are frozen, so tying and untying the boat can be a nightmare. With all that said, when Dylan first showed me the house and told me he wanted to buy it from his parents, I said, 'Hell, yeah!'" Dylan had purchased the island home from Karen and Charlie, who then moved onto the *Zarina*.

"So you don't have any apprehension about driving the boat?" I asked.

"Oh, no. I do it every day. I'm so used to it it's just not a big deal."

I had one opportunity to ride to town with Ashley during our stay, and she maneuvered her boat with incredible precision. It was a good thing, considering which slip she had. Docking her boat in town required the maritime equivalent of parallel parking the vessel while avoiding a bank of rocks, barnacle-covered pilings, and other boats. It was hard to imagine boat driving with as much familiarity as I consider driving a car. "Do you want me to deckhand for you or something?" I'd asked. "Should I be ready to jump on the dock and hold the lines?"

"I just want you to stay exactly where you are," she'd answered. I received similar requests *not* to help when it came to docking and tying up the boat from my husband throughout the trip. I took this to mean that if I didn't participate, we had less chance for calamity.

Our day of sunshine sadly came to an end, by which time the children were tuckered out and the majority of the adults were fairly pickled.

"That was so much fun," said Ashley. "Thanks for hosting and letting us crash this awesome little cove you have. It's so cool that it's protected like that, and it's perfect for the kids."

"Are you kidding? Thank *you*," I said. "This day would not have happened without you. We should do it again!"

Ashley and the other Sitkans laughed. I wasn't sure if it was the champagne or if I'd said something truly funny.

"Unfortunately," said Ashley, "we're not going to see another day like this for a *long* time."

* * *

New Archangel Dancers

The New Archangel Dancers take their name from Sitka's century-old designation as the capital of Russian America.

—Sitka Convention & Visitors Bureau

I have a lot of badass friends, but if had to rate them on their degree of badassedness (pronounced bad-ASS-ed-ness), my mother-in-law would be right there at the top. And I'm not just talking about her when she was young but also the current version of her. She's a seventy-year-old, margarita-drinking Zumba teacher. Her long history of badassedness includes, during her time in Sitka, being an original member of the New Archangel Dancers.

In 1969, cruise ships began touring through Southeast Alaska. Sitkans were eager to find a way to entertain, and capitalize on, the influx of tourists. A dance troupe seemed a viable option, and with the area's history of Russian influence, Russian folk dance emerged as the frontrunner. So a group of eight women, including my mother-in-law, formed the New

Archangel Dancers.

When one wants to form a group of Russian folk dancers, it helps to have a friendly neighborhood bishop of your local Russian Orthodox Church around. The Sitka dancers had Bishop Theodosius, who resided in Sitka from 1967 to 1972. In 1969, Theodosius lived in what was once a Russian orphanage. He taught the would-be dancers both the male and female parts for four dances, with accompanying Russian folk music he had on 8-track tapes. The New Archangel Dancers were off and running.

It's interesting to note that Theodosius wasn't simply a spiritual leader in small-town Alaska. The Orthodox Church in America names him "The Most Blessed Theodosius, Former Archbishop of Washington, Metropolitan of All America and Canada."[5] A little research and education in church lingo confirms that this makes him a big deal. Not just anyone gets to be a Metropolitan, and he continued rocking his position by meeting with world leaders to advise them on political and religious affairs. Theodosius retired in 2002, but I'm willing to bet he never forgot teaching Russian folk dances to eight young women in Sitka.

At one of the early performances of the New Archangel Dancers, a spectator gave them the contact information for a man who ran a Russian folk dance group in New York. The Sitkans brought him to Alaska for a visit so that they could learn from him and further expand their repertoire. He would be one of many resources the dancers used over the years, not only for help with the dances but also for knowledge and assistance with costumes.

Through all of this, the dancers remained an all-female group. When first formed, the New Archangel Dancers didn't have any men interested in joining. Later, when some of the Sitkan men realized that in addition to rehearsals and performances, the New Archangel Dancers threw legendary parties and had international travel plans in the works, they asked to join. Their request was politely declined.

Because it's an all-women group, some of the women had to play the male parts in the dances, which was anything but easy. If you picture Russian folk dancing, at some point you probably have an image of a man with his arms folded across his chest, squatting low to the ground, and alternately kicking his legs out in front of him. This move is called a *prisyadka* (присядка in Russian), and whoever came up with it was surely a masochist, because the human body is not naturally inclined to such feats.

If you were to ask any of the original dancers what they called this particular move, they'd reply with "front kick," "*pozinuke*," or "*puzinuk*." I understand calling them front kicks, but when I tried to verify the other names they came up with, I fell short. My best guess is that the ladies went out for a few cocktails after learning the terminology, and the word somehow devolved from *prisyadka* into *pozinuk*. The *p* and *k* stayed put, but they made the rest of the word their own.

Whatever nicknames exist for the *prisyadka*, I'm convinced that if I tried it, I'd topple back on my butt before completing a single kick, or somehow manage to injure an unrelated part of my body.

How'd you break your nose, Amanda?

I tried to do a leg kick. Obviously.

My mother-in-law, however, often played the male roles and executed this and other difficult moves. Like I said: badass.

In 1971, Alaska Airlines announced that it would be

infusing Russian culture into its brand. The stewardesses (because there were few stewards and because this was before we used the more politically correct and gender neutral "flight attendants") would wear Russian garb and serve tea from a samovar at the end of every in-flight meal. To celebrate the new campaign, the New Archangel Dancers were invited to perform on behalf of Alaska Airlines at a convention in Whitehorse, the capital city of Yukon in Northern Canada. After their appearance, the invitations kept coming, and the New Archangel Dancers' performances took them as far as Mexico, Japan, and, fittingly, Russia.

Both my mother-in-law's and Karen's badass designations have been earned from far more than just their involvement with the dancers. For instance, they've hiked the Alps, because I guess some people retire and take up knitting, and others hike the Alps. There's nothing wrong with knitting, of course. I love knitters. I'm a huge fan of the scarf, and knitting needles scare me. They're fairly badass. I couldn't take up knitting because I'm sure I'd stab myself in the eye and ruin the scarf by bleeding all over it. I am asserting, however, that hiking the Alps might be *slightly* more badass by comparison.

My in-laws weren't in Sitka at the time of our visit with Emilia and Ivy, and both my mother-in-law and Karen had long since retired from the New Archangel Dancers, but we wanted to take the girls to see the show nonetheless. The organization is going on fifty years and now has far more than eight dancers, and it's incredible to think that my mother-in-law was one of the originals.

"Holy crap, what the hell is that?" Mike asked as we parked behind his old high school in the lot of an enormous, state-of-the-art performance center.

"Apparently, it's the Sitka Performing Arts Center," I said. "I take it this wasn't here when you were in high school."

"No, we didn't have anything like this. It's awesome."

"Well, Dad," said Emilia. "It has been a *long* time since you were in high school. I mean, that was like, *back in the day*."

We exited the truck into a light rain and walked toward the building.

"Look at that pretty girl!" Ivy squealed. A woman in full costume held the door open for us. "You're very pretty," Ivy said as we walked in.

"Well, thank you," she replied. "You're very pretty, too."

We paid our admission and headed into the enormous theater.

"Can we sit up front?" Emilia asked.

"We sure can," I answered. A few seats were taken here and there, but the majority of them were empty. We settled into the first row.

"How long is this show?" Mike asked.

"Just a half hour." I checked the time on my phone. "And it should be starting soon."

After a minute, another dancer in costume emerged from the wings with a microphone in hand.

"Welcome, everyone," she said. "We're going to wait just a few minutes, as we had a ship come in late, but the passengers are on the bus and on their way here right now." Sitkans who cater to tourists are accustomed to tailoring their schedules around those of cruise ships.

When the awaited attendees arrived and filed into the auditorium, we looked around to find that our family of four was by far the minority.

"Is it just me or are there a lot of grandmas and grandpas

here?" Emilia asked loudly.

"Yeah," Ivy agreed. "Everyone is really *old*."

"And hopefully hard of hearing," I said.

The lady with the microphone emerged again to tell us the history of the New Archangel Dancers and that the day's program included six dancers in six dances. The theme of the dances generally involved flirtation. A female dropping a handkerchief and then the males fighting over it, or young people each taking a turn to dance in the center of the floor, preening and showing off their goods in hopes of attracting a member of the opposite sex. I happen to have spent a chunk of time in Russia as a teenager, during a semester of high school and a semester of college. I saw a lot of flirting between the sexes, though it more likely involved a bottle of vodka than a handkerchief. (I'm not trying to perpetuate a stereotype, and I've heard in the two decades since my last visit that consumption of vodka has gone down considerably, but when I was there, I saw a lot of people consuming unhealthy amounts of vodka. Sometimes I was one of them.)

After three dances, while the dancers changed costumes backstage, a young woman sang Alaska's state song while a man next to her held the Alaskan flag. I'm from Maryland, but I don't recall growing up with any knowledge of the state flag. It's an incorporation of two coats of arms of George Calvert, the first Lord Baltimore. I had to look it up. Alaskans know their flag's history and have great reverence for it. Maybe because it doesn't date back very far.

A contest to design Alaska's state flag was held in 1927, and thirteen-year-old Benny Benson won for his design of a blue background, the Big Dipper, and the North Star. For winning the design contest, he received a gold watch and

$1,000 to fund a trip to Washington, DC. It's a nice story, sort of. Some of the details of Benny's life are a little sad. His mother died when he was three, and he grew up in an orphanage, never made it to Washington, and instead later used the money to fund an education in diesel engine repair. He had a leg amputated and died of a heart attack before reaching sixty. The more depressing details of Benny's life are excluded from what they teach the schoolchildren in Alaska, and I first learned the rosier version of the story after having children, when my mother-in-law gave me a copy of *How Alaska Got Its Flag* to read to my daughters. Seeing the flag so honored was touching, in light of Benny's story.

The dancers performed their remaining three dances, and the girls were enthralled. During the last dance, the performers began a rhythmic clapping that starts slow and picks up tempo. This is very typical in Russian performances but a practice I lament. I have yet to meet a person as rhythmically uncoordinated as myself. In such situations, I look like a grump and a killjoy if I don't clap along. But if I join in, I'm inevitably off from the rest of the crowd. It's as if everyone else in the room shares a common language I never learned.

To hide my ineptitude, sometimes I fabricate another task to occupy my hands. I'm rooting around in my purse with urgency, as if my life depends on locating ChapStick, or buttoning and unbuttoning my coat as if constantly on the verge of either hypothermia or heat exhaustion. It would probably be better to be the weirdo with no rhythm than the crazy lady with her head in her purse or the freak show who keeps buttoning and unbuttoning her coat. In the Sitka Performing Arts Center, I attempted to join in with the clapping, and while I couldn't seem to clap at the same time as the rest of the crowd, neither was I alone. I looked to my right where Emilia sat, also out of sync with the crowd but at least in time with me.

"You are *so* my daughter," I whispered to her. I doubt she knew why I said such a thing, but she smiled nonetheless.

After the show, as we shuffled out of the auditorium alongside the cruise ship passengers, I whispered to Mike, "They didn't do the dance right."

"What do you mean?" he asked.

"You know that move your mom used to do as a dancer, the one where she'd squat low and kick her legs out in front of her?"

"Yeah."

"They used their arms to brace themselves, to prop themselves up. Their hands were behind them on the floor. Didn't your mom used to do it the real way, with her arms folded across her chest?"

"Yeah, she did."

I didn't fault the current dancers for doing a modified version. Even when I was young and fit and athletic, I'm not sure I could have ever done such as thing as a true *prisyadka*.

"But you know my mom," Mike said.

"Yes," I agreed. "*Total* badass."

* * *

Birds of Prey

*Raptors form lasting pair bonds and are considered monogamous –
which means they have one mate. However, researchers are working
to determine whether it's actually the mate or the nest site
that holds the strongest loyalty.*

—Alaska Raptor Center

"Let's just take a drive up Harbor Mountain Road," Mike
said.

"Because it's such a nice day for a drive?" I asked. The
four of us sat in the pickup truck, parked at the Crescent
Harbor marina. We looked out over the boats bobbing in their
slips under a relentless, thick rain. We'd come to town to stave
off cabin fever.

"Well, that's the point," Mike explained. "If we drive up
Harbor Mountain, we might be able to get above the clouds.
It's really cool to get above the rain and find sunshine up
there."

"All right," I said. "If there's light at the end of the tunnel,
I'm game."

We wound up Harbor Mountain, and I expected sunshine

at every turn.

"Why does it look so different over there?" Ivy asked.

"There was a landslide there last year," Mike explained.

"Oh my god!" I said.

"*Gosh*, Mom," said Emilia. "Say 'Oh my *gosh*!'"

"Sorry." The earth was unlike anything I'd seen before. A landslide does not yield a smooth path of earth but rather a giant swath of churned mud, speckled with rocks, uprooted trees, and jagged, menacing tree limbs.

"Well, I hope nobody was on the mountain when that happened," Emilia said.

"Actually, there were people there, and some of them were killed," Mike confirmed.

"That's so sad," said Ivy.

"Why did it happen?" asked Emilia.

"There was so much rain that it weakened the slope of the earth," Mike explained.

"But it's raining *now*," said Emilia.

"When the landslide happened, it rained way more than usual," Mike said. "This is normal Sitka weather; there's nothing to worry about. So, let's go see if we can find some sunshine."

It was a somber ride as we continued up the mountain, and I realized how foreign my husband's hometown was to me, this place of landslides, tsunami warnings, and bear awareness.

As we reached the end of the road and parked, we found ourselves still firmly in the rain and clouds.

"There's a trail right over there," Mike said. "Let's try it."

"Wait, are you making us go on a family hike in the rain?" Emilia asked as we exited the vehicle.

"It's not a full hike," Mike insisted, "just a short walk along this trail to see if we can get above the clouds." My eyes traveled up the trail, and I knew the likelihood of finding sunshine was slim.

"And look, girls!" I said. "We can eat blueberries along the way!" Wild blueberry bushes grew everywhere.

I plucked berries and tried to hand them to the girls, but they shook their heads and said in unison, "No, thanks."

The sound of the rain on our jackets was a steady, satisfying tap, but it didn't wane no matter how far up the trail we ventured.

"How long do we have to walk in the rain?" Ivy asked.

"I guess we can turn back. But it's just really cool when it happens, and I was hoping to show you guys," Mike said. "Sometimes when you come up here, you're above the clouds that are raining on Sitka, and it's really neat."

"Okay," said Emilia. "I'm going back to the truck now."

"But it's kind of cool, right?" asked Mike. "I mean, we're in a rain forest."

"I know, Dad," she replied. "I'm still going back to the truck."

"Don't worry, honey." I patted Mike on the arm. "I think it's cool."

The Tongass National Forest *is* a wonder. At 17 million acres, it's the largest national forest in the United States, encompasses Southeast Alaska, and includes not only temperate rain forest but also fjords and glaciers.

"Are there other rain forestes we can go to where it's not so rainy?" Ivy asked. She struggled with the plural of "forests," which came out more like "forestes." It's endearing, partly because I've heard my husband make the same mispronunciation, without the excuse of being six years old.

Three rainy days later, our friend Levi was in town. A ship pilot, Levi's job often takes him to the islands of Southeast Alaska, including his hometown of Ketchikan. When we found out he'd be in Sitka for a few hours, we jumped at the chance to meet up with him and arranged to do so at the Back Door coffeehouse behind Old Harbor Books. I ordered coffee for the adults and, for the girls, hot chocolate, which was delivered with whipped cream, sprinkles, and a tiny plastic giraffe mired in the whipped cream. Ivy squealed with delight.

As Mike and Levi got reacquainted, I tried to be a part of the conversation but also felt pulled in the direction of my daughters, who couldn't contain themselves in the presence of hot chocolate that was accompanied by not only whipped cream and sprinkles but also a small toy.

"This is so good," said Emilia, her mouth rimmed in whipped cream.

"Can you please use a napkin?" I scolded.

"Mmm, yummy," said Ivy, licking off every speck of sugar from the plastic giraffe.

"She'll suck on anything," Emilia said loudly.

"Stop that," I said, and took the giraffe from Ivy. "Emilia, quiet down."

My well-behaved daughters, like all children, occasionally utter regrettable phrases. They are especially prone to doing so with increased volume when we find ourselves in tiny, crowded places, like the Back Door coffee shop, and in the presence of old friends.

"How are your kids doing, Levi?" I asked.

"Good," he answered. "I don't know if you remember, but the last time I saw you guys, we were potty training."

We'd visited Levi and his family at their home on the Sunshine Coast in Australia. I remembered Levi's son, a toddler at the time, in the midst of being changed from swim trunks to dry clothes. At the point of nudity, the boy suddenly began peeing. Levi reacted by picking up his son and rushing to the bathroom. The urination continued, causing the floor in front of him to become slippery, at which point both Levi and his son went crashing to the floor. By the time they recovered and reached the toilet, his son no longer had to pee.

"We've almost got it down," Levi said. "But last week we were in a public bathroom at a urinal. I was trying to . . . demonstrate, you know, show him how you go. But before I could talk him through it, he looked in the urinal, said, 'Bubbles!' and reached in with his hands. So, that happened."

"Ah, parenthood," said Mike.

After coffee, the rain continued. We had just a few hours with Levi before he again had to pilot his ship, so Mike suggested we try Harbor Mountain once more.

"Wait, we have to go hike that mountain in the rain again?" Emilia asked.

"We didn't actually hike a mountain," Mike reasoned. "Let's just give it another try. Maybe there's sunshine at the top."

Once again we drove the winding road up the mountain, and once again we parked in the middle of a rain cloud. "Well, I guess it's not going to happen," Mike admitted. This time we refrained from exiting the vehicle, as the rain increased and I couldn't seem to tempt anyone with the promise of wild blueberries.

* * *

Two days later, the rain abated.

"Let's do something," I said. "Let's go see something. It's not raining!" It felt as if we'd been through forty days and nights of deluge.

"Can we go to the bird place?" Emilia asked. "I think we should, since I'm going to be an ornithologist."

"I'm going to be a waitress and a face painter," said Ivy.

"Do you want to go to the Raptor Center?" Mike asked me.

"Sure." I smiled. "For old times' sake."

The Alaska Raptor Center is home to raptors in various states of rehab. The Center is known for the treatment and care of bald eagles but has other raptors at the facility as well, including permanent residents who can't be released back into the wild, like Owlison, a great horned owl who recovered from a fracture but now has compromised flight capabilities, and Peek-a-Boo, a western screech owl hit by a car and now blind in one eye.

Then there's Jake, a red-tailed hawk who was taken from his nest as a chick and raised by a thirteen-year-old boy for the first four months of his life. Why it took the boy's parents four months to realize this wasn't a great idea, I can't say. Maybe the boy kept the bird hidden from them, or maybe they thought stealing a red-tailed hawk chick was a good idea. After all, it was a free pet that didn't require daily walks. And how hard could raising a hawk really be? It's not like it was a wild animal stolen from nature. Oh wait, that's exactly what it was. Maybe the boy had learned of falconry and thought he was ready for his own predator. What could be more fun and wholesome than hunting squirrels, bats, and pigeons with your very own hawk? In any case, Jake was eventually turned over to wildlife authorities, and though he's in perfect physical condition, he's what's called an imprint, never having had the opportunity to cultivate his innate abilities to live as a wild bird and completely dependent on humans for food.

The Sitka Raptor Center is a nonprofit, relying heavily on volunteer hours and consistent fundraising. The public can also "adopt" birds or patronize their gift shop. You can buy the usual suspects, like Sitka Raptor Center mugs and T-shirts, but also less common souvenirs like Sitka Raptor Center salad tongs or a Sitka Raptor Center ulu. This is a traditional knife used by the Inuit, Yupik, and Aleut. Blades can be anywhere from two inches to a foot long and apparently make popular souvenirs, as you'll find uluit (ulu in the plural form) for sale in just about every gift shop in town (often baring a brand or logo on the handle). I've purchased a wide variety of souvenirs and gifts during my travels, but it's never occurred to me to bring back a giant knife, no matter how unique or culturally significant. I'll take salad tongs or a jellyfish lava lamp over a blade any day.

In the Flight Training Center, rehabilitated eagles have room to test their wings as they relearn how to fly. The Raptor Center can't release eagles back into the wild until they can fly, but the eagles can't regain their flight capabilities without sufficient room to practice. Perches at various heights allow the birds to hone these skills, while visitors to the Center can observe through large windows.

"This is pretty impressive," I said to Mike as we watched eagles swoop back and forth over waterfalls, a stream, and pond.

"I bet cleaning it is no picnic."

"Right," I agreed. "Not just feathers and bird poop but

fish remains."

"I think I want to work here," Emilia declared.

"I don't remember this from the last time we were here," Mike said.

"It must be a new addition."

"You guys have been here before?" Emilia asked.

"Oh, yes," I answered. "Your dad and I once had a big party here."

"Ooh, that would be awesome," said Ivy.

"I want to have my birthday party here," said Emilia.

"Well," I said, "I think after the last time your dad and I were here, they stopped letting people have parties at the Raptor Center."

"Why?" Emilia asked. "What did you guys do?"

"Nothing much," Mike mumbled. He looked at me as if hoping to change the subject.

"What?" I asked. "You don't think they're old enough to learn what a keg stand is?"

* * *

I Do

Mawage. Mawage is wot bwings us togeder today. Mawage, that
bwessed awangment, that dweam wifin a dweam . . .

—*The Princess Bride* (1987)

My husband and I take full responsibility if the Raptor Center no longer rents out its large hall for events. It started with a phone call.

"So, Amanda and I are going to get married," Mike told his parents. We'd been together for a year and a half and, at the seasoned ages of twenty-one and twenty-two, decided it was time to get hitched. I heard faint sounds of excitement and congratulations coming from the phone receiver that he held to his ear. "Yeah, we're talking about eloping. I think we're just going to go to Vegas."

We abhorred the idea of a lavish wedding. I was never the little girl who dreamed about that special day, nor would I consider spending thousands of dollars on a dress. We were living in California at the time, I waiting tables while Mike was finishing up school, and driving to Vegas for a quickie wedding was all the fanfare we needed. We didn't realize that if you're planning on eloping, you're not supposed to tell anyone about it until after the fact. Mike's parents pleaded with us not to elope.

"Why don't they want us to elope?" I asked Mike.

"They really want to be there when we get married," he said.

"Oh. Why? It's not like we're going to do the big wedding or anything."

"They know that. They just want to be a part of it."

"Huh."

Over the course of many follow-up phone conversations, they talked us into flying to Alaska to get married.

"Okay, but no guests," I insisted. "We don't need a whole bunch of people staring at us. Let's keep this shit simple." It's not that I'm not romantic, I just have a very low threshold for sentimentality.

We journeyed to Alaska where my mother-in-law had made all of the arrangements, including location, officiant, flowers, reception, cake, and a place for us to stay while there.

She also arranged for me to have my hair done in town on the day of the wedding.

"That's awesome," I said. "Because it's not one of my better skills."

In a small salon, a high-pitched, petite woman whose only expression was an ear-to-ear smile styled my hair.

"I just don't want it too . . . big," I said. "I'm not really a big hair kind of person."

"Okay," she said enthusiastically. "We'll have you looking gorgeous in no time."

She shampooed, conditioned, dried, curled, and coiffed. I was facing away from the mirror but became concerned near the end when she grabbed the hair spray. I'm quite certain that she turned my head into a fire hazard with the amount of shellac she applied. When I stood up from the chair, would I topple to the ground under the weight of lacquered hair? It was a genuine concern. She ceased spraying, but I was afraid to breathe or open my eyes for fear of the cloud of Aqua Net hovering around my face. I felt the chair whirl around to face the mirror. Fearful but curious, I opened my mouth and eyes at the same time to find the Bride of Frankenstein version of myself staring back in horror. The height of my hair was impressive.

"Wow," I said.

"Do you like it?" she squealed.

"It's so . . . big. And pretty." My eyes began welling with tears. I think she assumed they were tears of joy. "Thank you so much."

Ten minutes later, I was outside of the salon, desperately trying to squash the solid helmet of hair.

"It's not that bad," Mike said weakly.

"I don't even want to be seen like this," I cried. "And don't let me near an open flame. I'm a human torch soaked in lighter fluid. I swear I'll go up in flames in half a second."

After fifteen painful minutes in a public restroom with a hairbrush, I'd tamed the beast as best I could. After a pint of Guinness, I stopped crying.

An hour later, Charlie shuttled us by boat from Sitka to nearby Berry Island. My decree of "no guests" wasn't entirely accurate, but aside from ourselves and the officiant, the only attendees were Mike's parents, my mother and then-stepfather, and a photographer. I figured that was *plenty*.

At the dock, we were met by the island's owners, a kind, quiet couple who allowed us the use of their island for our wedding. They led us along a forested path through the island to a clearing with an intricately built studio home, which included a deck overlooking the water.

Because of space limitations, Mike and I dressed for the wedding at the same time in the tiny bathroom, bucking all traditions of the groom not seeing the bride before she walks down the aisle. We didn't have an aisle, in any case. We awkwardly elbowed each other as we readied ourselves.

"Could you zip me up?" I asked Mike, referring to the off-white dress I'd purchased at a shopping mall.

"Sure thing. Can you hand me my shoes?"

"Here you go," I said. "Are we late? Is there a set time when we're supposed to do this?"

"I don't think so. I think it's just pretty much whenever we're ready. You really want me to wear these suspenders?"

"I do. I think suspenders are totally hot."

"Okay," he said doubtfully. "Should we go get married now?"

"Yeah, let's do this."

Our officiant was a woman named Marilyn Hanson, which I've always remembered because it's so close to Marilyn Manson. She presented us with three printed versions of the service from which we could choose.

"Is there one without God involved?" I asked. "That's the one I want."

The ceremony was a few minutes of emotion so intense and exciting that I focused really hard on not wetting myself. That possibility reinforced the value of not standing in front of a few hundred people. With the hitching complete, we uncorked champagne bottles, posed for pictures, and reveled in the idyllic setting. After an hour, everyone else traveled back to town for the night while Mike and I had the home to ourselves. Mike's parents had packed us a gourmet basket, including marinated filet mignon to cook on the grill, strawberries, more champagne, and other treats. Their efforts and generosity were a good indication of what a future with them as in-laws would be like.

The next day, Charlie returned to retrieve us from the island, and that evening the reception took place at the Raptor Center. This was the big party for everyone who was pissed off at not having been invited to the actual wedding. At least that's what I thought at the time. I would later learn that far more people than just those in Sitka were pissed off at the exclusion. We had friends and relatives across the United States who would have traveled to Sitka for the event if we'd had guests at the ceremony, and the lack of invitations stung more people than I'd have thought. This never occurred to me ahead of time, that others would feel it their right to watch us say "I do." I equate the experience with giving birth. There are people who bring their extended families into the delivery room, but I'm the type of person who'd rather cut off her big toe than make it a public celebration. Though many didn't (and still don't) understand why we had our wedding the way we did, I have no regrets.

The reception included a buffet, the jewel of which was a thirty-five-pound king salmon I'd caught when a family friend took us fishing two days prior. I say I caught it, as if the fisherman who took us out on his boat, equipped us, and told me exactly what to do, step by step, from reeling it in to gutting it, had nothing to do with it. True fisherman are used to giving up the glory.

I caught a glimpse of the prepared salmon in between introductions.

"So which one was yours?" my mom asked. "Which fish did you catch?"

"Mom," I answered, "those are two filets of one fish."

Her face took on the expression of one who realizes she's asked a less than intelligent question.

"Oh, crap," she said. "Please forget I ever said that."

Along with the buffet, there was music, dancing, and a keg of Alaskan Amber. I was introduced to dozens of people I didn't know while Mike reconnected with high school classmates, friends, and people he pretended to remember. By the time Mike and I had properly greeted everyone, the food was gone, and the event had fully transformed from reception to wild party. I knew it deserved that designation when the keg stands began. I'm not sure of the point of drinking beer upside down, but apparently it's a thing. You place your hands on the rim of the keg, someone holds your feet in the air, and someone else pours beer in your mouth. The inversion is meant to either heighten the experience or an attempt at drowning the imbiber. I did a keg stand, Mike did a keg stand, all his friends did a keg stand, and then our parents did them. We drank without drowning, and there was laughter and music and many people talking far louder than necessary. But that's what happens at parties.

"Apparently one of the Raptor Center employees just told my mom we need to keep the noise level down," Mike told me.

"Really? We're being too loud?"

"I guess we're disturbing the birds."

"Oh, right. Well, what did your mom say?"

"She told them we'd try but also that it's a wedding reception. I mean, what did they expect?"

"Maybe they assumed we were aspiring ornithologists and not keg stand practitioners."

The nature of our event hadn't been hidden from Raptor Center staff when my mother-in-law secured the place, but I guess they failed to consider that wedding receptions involve music and noise and that the birds wouldn't appreciate such a thing. I regret the stress we caused the birds, but they all survived the night just fine. All the same, I'm pretty sure that ever since that night, the Raptor Center hasn't rented their facility to any group whose event involves a keg of beer.

* * *

Battle of the Bilge

The sea, the snotgreen sea, the scrotumtightening sea.

—James Joyce

The Alaskan dawn in summer arrives before 5 a.m. This is wonderful for early risers, the chance to greet the day as it is born, to accomplish what might otherwise be procrastinated. If the rain relents and the sun shines, it's a beautiful time to witness the full glory of the Alaskan landscape. That's one way to look at it.

Mike is an early riser anyway. To be able to wake at 4:30 or 5 a.m. without the need of an alarm is a wondrous thing to him. I, on the other hand, secretly wished we had blackout curtains. In Alaska, I either woke early with the morning sun and couldn't go back to sleep or, on overcast days, would try to wake up, but the sound of rain would pull me back under like a lullaby. I'd try to open my eyes, but the sound of each drop of rain on the roof pressed down on my eyelids. There was no middle ground. Waking was either butt-crack-of-dawn early or a struggle, as if I'd been shot in the face with a tranquilizer dart, stretched out over an hour and a half.

On a day of promising weather, I resolved to take our paddleboard out for the afternoon and get a little exercise. I'd previously paddleboarded only in our small, protected cove, while Mike had paddled beyond to open water and completely circled the island on more than one occasion.

Mike and I are not a competitive couple. There is no one-upmanship or gloating in our marriage, but we are often inspired by one another. All of which is a tactful way of saying that if he was going to routinely and *casually* paddle around an entire island, surely I could complete the same journey at least once, damn it.

Today's the day, I thought. *I'm going all the way around*. There was no way to get lost; I'd just hug the shore until I arrived back at my starting point. Most people wouldn't need to voice this strategy to themselves, but I'm notorious for getting lost, and my default direction is whichever way is wrong. I envisioned the headlines: "Directionally Challenged Woman Lost at Sea" or "Idaho Mother of Two Unable to Travel in a Circle."

I left Mike in charge of the girls and took the paddleboard out for some much-needed time alone. Paddling on my knees out of the cove, I reached open water and tentatively stood up. I was *pretty* sure I wouldn't fall off . . . unless I was thrown off balance by the wake of a passing vessel. Or a whale that decided to breach underneath me; that would be just my luck. Or a sea lion that would tip my board just to be an asshole. And if I did fall off, did I know how to get back on? Would hoisting myself back up require upper-body strength, which I did not possess? What if the paddle drifted away? What if the *board* drifted away? I lowered back down to my knees, paddled back to shore, and went inside the house.

"Back so soon?" Mike asked.

"No, I'm going back out. I just want to grab one of the kids' life jackets. I mean, I'm totally fine, but I want to go all the way around the island, and I think I'll feel more confident if I have a life jacket." We had adult life jackets but kept them on the boat at the dock on the other side of the island.

"Okay," he said. "Good luck."

I set out for another try. With a life jacket, I was sure I'd have the confidence to do it. Chances were that I wouldn't have any interaction with sea life. In all likelihood, the worst that would happen would be that I'd fall off, lose the paddle, kick myself and the board back to shore, and find my way back to the house. Not the end of the world, because in this scenario I don't die. I put the life jacket on without clipping it. Not out of overconfidence or a blasé attitude toward water safety but because it was a life jacket designed for a seven-year-old girl. There was no possible way I was going to get that sucker closed. In fact, the life jacket was probably good for my posture, as it was so tight on my shoulders that it forced them back, and I couldn't help but think of Chris Farley singing "Fat Guy in a Little Coat" in *Tommy Boy*. I wondered how long it would take for the strain on circulation in my armpits to cause me to pass out. Or would it just deaden my limbs? Suddenly, the addition of a life jacket didn't mean much in terms of safety.

I paddled on my knees beyond the cove. The water was dark, though occasionally I could make out the tops of giant kelp forests. When their leaves reached the surface, I spotted tiny snails clinging to them. What if I got tangled in kelp?

Every movie scene of someone being grabbed by the ankle and pulled under or becoming entangled and drowning as a result flashed through my mind. I looked back to the island, so tiny when I was confined to it but now like its own country, one that seemed nearly impossible to circumnavigate. I pushed from my mind the fact that my husband routinely did exactly that in about fifteen minutes, start to finish. I looked back to the sea and saw the head of a sea lion poking up about fifty yards away. Something about that sea lion's expression convinced me that it was a complete asshole, as far as sea lions go.

"Well, that was fun," I said aloud to no one and paddled back to the safety of the protected cove.

"How was it?" Mike asked when I returned.

"Great," I lied.

"Did you make it around the island?"

"Yeah, not so much."

"You look kind of funny," Mike said, referring to the life jacket pinning back my shoulders.

As I struggled to remove it, I looked at my husband and said, "If you start singing 'Fat Guy in a Little Coat,' I will physically harm you." He laughed, and I realized he hadn't had that image in his head until I planted it there.

My intention had been to exercise while also reassure myself that I was still somewhat on par with my husband when it came to physical aptitude and a willingness to test it. Without any sense of competition, of course. But instead all I'd accomplished was getting my husband to equate me with Chris Farley. I love Chris Farley. His death still saddens me. But when I think of my husband and celebrities he most resembles, I come up with Emilio Estevez and Viggo Mortensen. When my husband thinks of my celebrity doppelganger, he's now forever plagued with refrains of "Fat Guy in a Little Coat."

"What are we having for dinner, Mom?" Ivy asked.

"Tacos!" I removed the life jacket (with considerable effort and to my great relief). I wanted nothing more than to make dinner. It was something useful that I could complete, and I was *good* at it. It would temper my paddleboarding failure.

"Yes!" Ivy yelled. "I love tacos."

"Ooh, we're having tacos? I love tacos, too," Emilia said. "But wait, you're not making us eat fish tacos, are you?" The scars of the rockfish experience had not yet faded.

"No," I said. "We're having beef. I'll start cooking now."

"You're the best mom ever!" Ivy cheered.

"Yes, I am!" I agreed.

Ivy often proclaims that I am the best mom ever. This can be the result of tacos, anything containing sugar, or allowing her to help unload the dishwasher.

I opened the fridge and removed a plastic bag. I'd taken frozen ground beef from the freezer that morning to defrost. When I opened the bag, however, I realized that I'd mistakenly defrosted bait. The bag held the leftover squid we'd used when fishing. The beef remained frozen solid in the freezer.

"Crap," I said. "We're not having tacos tonight."

* * *

The next day, we headed for the boat as our break from the rain came to an end. It started as a light drizzle when we reached the dock.

"Is it supposed to look like that?" I asked, motioning to our tiny vessel. Inches of water sloshed in the back, something I hadn't noticed before.

"Huh," said Mike. "It looks like the bilge isn't working."

He fiddled with a valve at the stern. "But I can't seem to figure out why."

"Does this mean we'll sink?" I asked, because I like to get the worst-case scenario out of the way right off the bat.

"I think we'll be fine. Just pull this little thing out while we're going." At the mention of "little thing," he indicated the valve he'd fiddled with earlier.

"Um, okay. And I'll just go ahead and put on my *adult-sized* life jacket, which perfectly fits my frame and in which I do not look ridiculous."

As we motored away from the dock, I did as Mike instructed. I must have been really good at my job, the pulling of the "little thing," because water fled the boat immediately, and I was 72 percent sure that we would make it to town without sinking.

We saw four sea lions along the way, slowing down on occasion to get a better view of them.

"I used to think of them as cute and cuddly," I said.

"Don't be silly, Mom," Emilia scolded. "They're wild animals. And you should never approach a wild animal. Do you understand?"

"Got it."

We pulled into the marina at low tide. The breakwater rocks along the harbor were striated, a nautical palette of sorts. The bottom level was mottled yellow and brown, covered with seaweed and barnacles. Above this was a strip of clear gray rock, the bridge between the growth below and above water. A green layer of algae-covered rock hovered atop the breakwater. As we passed the breakwater rocks, the maritime equivalent of a street sign read, "No Transient Vessels Allowed."

The rain thickened, but you cannot hide indoors in a part of the world where it rains more than not. Sitka's average annual rainfall is 131 inches.[6] That's almost eleven feet of rain. Sitkans utter a depressing and unsympathetic chuckle when they hear their southern Seattle neighbors complain about wet weather (Seattle averages 37 inches or just over three feet[7]). As such, we donned our rain jackets and set about our errands around town. In the course of doing so, we saw young mothers pushing strollers, kids playing basketball and pushing others on swing sets, all as the rain poured down. It was an odd sight given my childhood. I grew up in Maryland, where a fair drizzle was cause for gluttonous meal delivery and movie marathons.

Later that afternoon, I contemplated these differences as we walked from the dock on Bamdoroshni back to our island home. I stared at my feet in an effort to remain surefooted and upright. The rain made the worn planks of the narrow walkway slick, and I was determined to focus on my footing to avoid falling. By looking down, I failed to see the branches of red huckleberries, weighed down by the rain and hanging head high, whereas before the deluge, I'd passed beneath them with little problem. I know that I walked into the red huckleberry branch, but it felt like the branch had assaulted me. As if it maliciously popped out of nowhere to smack me fully in the face. I was caught off guard; my head whipped back as my feet flew out in front of me, and I landed in a soggy thud directly on my rear. Mike and the girls were ahead of me. My husband had apparently seen the branch and avoided it, while Emilia and Ivy passed under entirely, despite its bowed state.

"Oh my gosh," Emilia and Ivy said in unison, turning around to see me sprawled out on the walkway. Their faces showed concern but also a concerted effort to subdue smiles and laughter.

"Are you okay?" Mike asked, trying not to smirk himself.

"I'm fine," I insisted, trying to get up without falling again.

"Did you hurt your . . . butt?" Emilia asked.

"You said 'butt.'" Ivy giggled. The word never ceases to be funny, and they spent the rest of the walk talking and laughing about my injured butt.

"If you don't stop laughing," I warned, "I'll feed you squid for dinner."

* * *

Skookum

The English language is nobody's special property.

—Derek Walcott

"Mom, what is that a picture of?" Emilia asked.
"Well, let's take a look and see what it says." A woman appeared to be blowing into something. I read the caption. "She's inflating a seal gut," I reported.

"Huh, that's interesting," she said, with not a hint of squeamishness.

"Why is she inflating a seal gut?" Ivy asked.

Before I could come up with a logical explanation as to the motivation for inflating a seal gut, Emilia jumped in. "You see, Ivy," she said, "they used all parts of the animal, and they have to dry it and prepare it before they can start sewing it. Like right here," she motioned to a nearby case, "we have an example. This is a seal gut parka."

We'd been in the Sheldon Jackson Museum less than ten

minutes. Had she really come to understand the applications of seal gut during that time? Or had she previously studied the art of native gut-skin outerwear and I just hadn't known about it? Either way, she was correct, and we learned that while we tend to think of native people as clad entirely in furs and leather, things like seal gut and fish skin were commonly used elements as well. I leaned in for another look at the photograph of the woman inflating a seal gut and resolved to never again complain about my domestic chores.

Artifacts at the Sheldon Jackson Museum come from the Aleut (hence the Aleutian Islands), Alutiiq, Yup'ik, Athabascan, Inupiat, Tlingit, Haida, and Tsimshian people. Staff at the museum are on hand not just to answer questions about these people and their artifacts but also to assist you in pronunciation when you get up the nerve to admit you have no idea how to form the words with which you are presented.

"What are those people doing?" Ivy asked. At two long tables, eight people concentrated intently on blocks of wood in front of them while a man walked around, viewing their work and offering guidance.

"It looks like they're taking some sort of class," I said.

In addition to woodcarving, the museum offers classes on masks, silver engraving, fish skin sewing, weaving, and other arts through a Native Artist Residency program.

"Do we get to do that?" Ivy asked.

"I don't think so, Ivy. It looks like that's just for adults. But let's go check out some of these exhibits."

We learned of the Last Potlatch in 1904, an attempt to endorse a final traditional ceremony of the Tlingit people, after which it was hoped that the Tlingit would abandon certain aspects of their culture. A potlatch is an elaborate native gathering, often described as involving large feasts, traditional dancing, and a meeting of clans. The gatherings were held to honor births, deaths, totem pole dedications, and other clan milestones. The Last Potlatch in Sitka in 1904 lasted four weeks. At first this seems excessive. I have never been one to shy away from celebrating. My inner glutton is happy to be first in line for the food at any ceremony, be it joyful or somber, but a month-long gathering would put my well-honed skills of overindulgence to the test. On the other hand, this was supposed to be the *last* potlatch. If you told me I could have a party but it would be my last, I'm pretty sure I'd rally and stretch that sucker into next year.

Luckily, the 1904 event wasn't truly the last one. A Centennial Potlatch was held in 2004 to commemorate the event of a hundred years prior and to firmly declare that preservation of culture and diversity are actually really good things.

"Mom, I want to do the scavenger hunt," Ivy said.

"Okay," I agreed. "But what are you talking about?" My daughters seemed to know the ins and outs of the museum as if they'd grown up there. I was entirely lost.

"It's right *here*, Mom," Ivy said with mild exasperation. She pointed to a stack of pamphlets on a table next to a series of stamps. The pamphlet had large blank spaces next to clues. We had to read the clue, figure out what artifact in the museum it referred to by sleuthing around, and then return to the table and stamp the corresponding stamp next to the clue. It is just the sort of thing I love to do, appealing to my inner nerd detective, and I was happy to oblige.

We learned about *baidarkas* (Aleutian kayaks), saw tools

that women used to clean skins and filet fish, and found out what a Tlingit warrior helmet looked like. When Ivy would let me, I'd stop to read some of the more detailed histories.

"They have great words," I said. "Hoochinoo is moonshine. That's just awesome. And *skookum* is really a word." Growing up on the East Coast, I'd never encountered the word skookum until I met my in-laws, who used it frequently. It's not that I don't trust my in-laws, I just don't trust anything my in-laws *say*. They are legendary for both their verbal flops and inventions.

My mother-in-law will request something from the "reefer." This is how she refers to the refrigerator, but for the longest time I thought she was asking me to grab a joint from a secret pot stash I was supposed to know about.

My husband, who frequently breaks into song, sometimes settles on "Swing Low, Sweet Cheerio." And my father-in-law believes that certain word pairings are interchangeable, like ammonia and pneumonia, or autopsy and biopsy, despite my assertion that his word choice will have a drastically different outcome on his meaning.

When Emilia claps her hands together and says, "Let's get this road on the show!" or "Oh, for the love of sake!" I know they've passed their gift on to her.

I was sure, when I first heard my in-laws use the term skookum, that it was their invention. I would later learn this wasn't the case. It's Chinook jargon with a range of meanings, including "large, powerful, and monstrous," though the one most Sitkans mean when they use the word is "good or excellent."

"Come on, Mom." Ivy tugged at my sleeve. "We have to find the caribou hide decorated with porcupine quills."

"Okay, sorry. I'm on board." As much as I like detective work, the museum's artifacts were overwhelming in scope. "Let's go see how Dad and Emilia are doing with theirs."

"How's it going?" Mike asked as we approached.

"This thing is hard," I said.

"I know," he agreed.

"We still need to find the ceremonial object made from mountain goat wool and cedar bark," Emilia said.

No prize awaited us for finishing the scavenger hunt. We wouldn't be graded for our efforts or shamed if we didn't complete the task, yet we still felt compelled to fill out the pamphlet in entirety.

"We'll show you ours if you show us yours," Emilia suggested. The four of us then set about covertly copying the answers from each other. When we were finished, I felt like I'd cheated on the SAT.

"I'm going to see if Emilia can interview one of the staff," Mike said.

Karen, a Yup'ik woman on staff who was happy to oblige, described how she had to leave her family and tribe after developing adult asthma. She'd moved to Sitka for a climate more conducive to her health, knowing no one upon arrival.

"You had to leave your family! That's so sad," Emilia said. She harped on the sadness of this for a full minute, and an image flashed in my mind of Emilia as a ruthless reporter set on bringing her interviewees to tears for the sensationalism of it. The interviewee in this case was a wonderful sport and deftly moved on when the chance presented itself.

She spoke of working with fish skin garments. "And back in the day," she told Emilia, "they used to tan the fish skin with the urine of a baby boy being breastfed by his mother."

I'd never have guessed the pee from breastfed little boys could be in high demand, but that shows you how much I know. Apparently the hormones of the breast milk and the boy passed a quality into the urine that could tan fish skin leather to the softness of rose petals. The urine of breastfed little girls wasn't mentioned, and I wondered if this had to do with the urine itself or because the difference in anatomy made it harder to collect.

Emilia didn't bat an eye and asked Karen if there was anything else she'd like to share. Karen spoke for another minute about characteristics of the Yup'ik people.

"Love and respect are a deep part of our culture," she said.

"Well, that wraps up another episode of 'Girl Around the World,'" Emilia said a little too quickly and as if she hadn't really been listening. "Thanks for joining me . . . uh . . . what was your name again?"

Karen was exceedingly gracious, thanked us for the opportunity, and took no note of Emilia's curt ending.

As we left the building, Emilia asked, "Did you know that this building was the first concrete structure in Alaska and it houses the oldest continuously operated museum in the state?"

"Um, no. I did not know that. How do you know so much about this place?" I asked.

"It says so right here on the pamphlet," she said.

"And this used to be Sheldon Jackson College," Mike said of the grounds and buildings surrounding the museum.

"Sheldon Jackson must have been the president or something," Ivy said.

Jackson was actually a Presbyterian missionary with considerable influence in Sitka, and as such, many places still bear his name. He was considered a humanitarian and took great interest in preserving the culture of the indigenous people, gathering many of the artifacts in the museum himself. In the late 1800s, he was also the general agent of education in the Alaskan Territory, determined to educate native children as well as their nonnative counterparts. This is admirable, though he also sought policy to forbid use of native languages, which seems at odds with his interest in preserving native culture.

"I feel like I learned a lot today," Emilia said.

"Me, too," I agreed.

"And I really want to try that seal gut thing," she added.

The rest of us remained silent.

* * *

Crapshooters and Hot Box Girls

Movies are a fad. Audiences really want to see live actors on a stage.

—Charlie Chaplin

"Why do they call it *Guys and Dolls*, Mom?" Ivy asked as we headed back to the Sitka Performing Arts Center, where we'd watched the New Archangel Dancers. "What do they mean by that?"

This was the first of many questions that let me know there'd be much explaining to do.

"Dolls just means girls. It's about guys and girls," Mike answered.

"Ugh," groaned Emilia. "I hope there isn't any kissing."

The show was the culmination of the Sitka Fine Arts Camp for teenagers. Aspiring young actors, stage managers, and set designers spend two weeks in Sitka (some are Sitkans, but most visit and stay in dormitories) preparing for their weekend of performances.

The performance was good but speckled with the awkwardness that accompanied the ages of the actors. One character was stiff as cardboard, moving as if with fused joints, reciting his lines in a robotic monotone. I leaned over to Mike and whispered, "I wonder why this kid got such a prominent part."

A minute later, the young actor in question broke into song, displaying a phenomenal singing voice. "That's why," Mike whispered back.

At intermission and after the play, Mike and I had to answer a few questions.

Ivy: "Why did the girl get so silly when she drank the drink the boy gave her?"

Me: "Too much of anything can make you sick and sometimes also silly." I held my breath, waiting for a comment about me after a few glasses of wine, but it mercifully never came.

Emilia: "What does shooting craps mean?"

Mike: "It's a type of gambling."

Emilia: "Is that what you guys are talking about when I hear you say 'crap'? Do you and Mom gamble? Are you going to go to jail?"

Me: "We'll try not to, sweetie."

Emilia: "But why do you guys talk about gambling?"

Me: "We don't. Crap is another word for poop. When we say, 'Oh, crap,' it's like saying, 'Oh, poop.'"

Ivy, trying it out: "Oh, crap."

Mike: "Please don't start using the word crap."

Emilia: "So shooting craps is about shooting poop? I don't get it. Adults are so weird."

Me: "It has nothing to do with poop. No one is shooting

poop."

Ivy: "Why'd the boys keep lying to the girls? That's just not nice."

Mike: "The boys liked the girls."

Ivy: "So they lied to them?"

Emilia: "Like I said, adults are weird."

Me: "It's a really complicated question, but you're right, Ivy. It's not nice."

Emilia: "Can I come to this theater camp when I'm a teenager?"

Mike: "Maybe. Let's see if you can earn the money to pay for it."

Emilia: "Okay. When we get back to Boise, I'm going to start selling my toys in the driveway."

Of all the things Emilia asks for, the opportunity to sell her toys in the driveway is one of the most frequent. This is an offshoot of a garage sale I did a few years ago. In light of the success we had, she doesn't understand why standing at the end of the driveway to flag down passing motorists in the hopes they'll cough up five dollars for thirty-seven pieces of a fifty-piece puzzle is not a sound business model.

We exited the theater to a forceful rain and stood under the entrance's shelter.

"Well, what now?" Mike asked.

"I want to do something," Emilia said.

Mike offered his go-to suggestion: "Push-ups?"

"No, Dad." She rolled her eyes.

"And I don't think we should go for a hike, either," Ivy said, looking bleakly out at the rain.

"But let's do something," Emilia reiterated.

Normally I chastise her for wanting to "do something"

immediately after we've taken her somewhere special. After all, we'd just treated them to a live musical. But in this case, I understood and felt the same.

The idea of heading straight back to the island was a depressing one. The seclusion of the island home was not necessarily a bad thing, but being cooped up inside, imprisoned by the relentless rain, bred claustrophobia. It was a growing toll on my sanity. I looked at Mike blankly.

"Should we go get some food?" he asked. There is nothing I like more in the world than going out to eat. It feeds my body and my gluttonous nature. While I love to cook and don't mind cleaning up after, these things are even more enjoyable with a periodic break from them when someone else does the work. After so much serving, I love to be served myself. I may have done a fist pump in response to Mike's suggestion, and I was clearly the most enthusiastic one of our group.

"There's a pizza place not far from the marina that's supposed to be really good," he said. "Should we check it out?"

"Well, now Mom's excited, so we sort of have to," Emilia answered. I'm like our family's Labrador. You can't make mention of a treat and then fail to deliver.

Mean Queen would turn out to be one of our favorite restaurants in Sitka. It's a place that Sitkans seem to have strong feelings about, one way or the other. For everyone we met who agreed, "Yeah, I love that place," there were others who contended, "The pizza's not very good, and it's pricey." Of these latter, I'm not sure what their benchmark for good pizza is, but I thought Mean Queen's was excellent. And as far as pricey, most things in Alaska are pricey to counter the cost of getting goods shipped there. In any case, we'd visit on more than one occasion. They had Guinness on tap, and the girls loved both the pizza and the Caesar salad. I was partial to the Imperial Pie while Mike enjoyed the Princess, which he's man enough to order without flinching.

"Is it going to rain forever in Alaska?" Ivy asked.

"No," said Mike. "I promise. In fact, it's actually supposed to clear up over the next few days."

"Awesome!" Emilia exclaimed. "We should go on an adventure!"

Mike and I looked at each other, debating whether or not to remind Emilia that she was, at that moment, in the middle of living an adventure.

"Let's go back out on Charlie and Karen's boat," Ivy suggested.

"It doesn't work that way," I chided. "We can't just invite ourselves out on their boat."

As we finished up our meal, which meant Mike and me devouring not only our own pizza but also the abandoned crusts left on our daughters' plates, I felt the familiar vibration of my phone in my pocket, indicating a new message. Our next adventure was in the works.

* * *

Parental Duties

According to a report from 2007, 78 percent of the large whale population in Southeast Alaska have scars indicating entanglement.

—Juneau Empire

"So we should drug the kids now?" I asked. "That came out wrong."

"Yes," Karen confirmed. "If you have Dramamine, I'd give it to them now."

"It's a few hours to Goddard," Charlie added. "And in a few minutes, it's going to start getting rough."

We were quick to accept Charlie and Karen's invite to another cruise on the *Zarina*, this time overnight. For a one-night stay, we had what seemed an unnecessary amount of belongings, which I waded through in search of the Dramamine. A family of four doesn't often travel light, on top of which we felt compelled to pack for more than one climate. Rain gear is always a must, but if the weather held and the clouds remained at bay, the beaches of Southeast Alaska could experience bikini weather. We also had plans to visit hot springs along the way. Thus, packing for the overnight trip necessitated warm-weather clothes, cold-weather clothes, rain gear, bathing suits, towels, life jackets, and pajamas. We also brought aboard a gigantic cooler filled with snacks, drinks, and food so that we could share meal duties. Having a substantial amount of luggage and a large cooler felt like a big deal when we brought everything aboard the *Zarina*, where space was already at a premium. I was inclined to apologize for every square inch we occupied.

"I found the Dramamine," I said.

We crushed the tablets and gave them to the kids in spoonfuls of yogurt.

"You don't have to put mine in yogurt, Mom," Ivy said. "Next time, can I just take the pill?"

"Why?" I asked.

"Because I just really like taking pills. It's so much fun."

"You're just saying that because I'm not good at it," said Emilia.

"Yes," I agreed. "Can we stop with the poorly masked, passive-aggressive one-upmanship over your sister?"

"Huh?"

"Just be nice."

After consuming the Dramamine-laced yogurt, the girls retreated to the lower bunk where they'd sleep later that night and promptly fell into a nap that would last for hours and the length of the trip to Goddard. This was a good thing, as within minutes the *Zarina* rocked steeply from side to side.

"Whoa," I said, steadying myself between the galley counter and table. "You weren't kidding."

"I've had to learn the hard way what needs to be secured,"

said Karen. "Our first trip out, I was sure I'd battened down the hatches. Sure enough, the fridge flew open, we broke glasses, it was a mess."

"It's going to be rough like this for a while," Charlie informed us from the captain's chair.

When the sea eventually calmed, I relented my grip (which I'd kept continually so that if anything did go flying, at least it wouldn't be me) and spent some time taking in the scenery. We spied eagles and sea otters, trolled unsuccessfully for king salmon and coho, and listened on the radio as the Coast Guard issued reports on an entangled whale. As soon as I heard this, I imagined us racing to the whale, where I'd jump in the frigid waters and bravely untangle the whale myself. The whale would sense the purity of my intentions and allow me to do my good deed, after which it would let me ride around on its back as a reward for my efforts before delivering me safely back to the *Zarina*. Sadly, this did not happen.

By the time we reached Goddard, the girls were hazily awake and excited about the prospect of visiting the hot springs.

"So, I guess we can't just pull ashore," I said, noting the less than welcoming shoreline.

"No," Karen confirmed. "It's a little trickier than that."

The *Zarina* towed a small skiff for just such instances. But because of the rocky shoreline at Goddard, there wasn't a place to pull the skiff ashore, either. We anchored the *Zarina* offshore and piled into the skiff with towels, snacks, and swimsuits, and Charlie motored us toward land. In a few inches of water, all but Charlie hopped out of the skiff and trudged to shore, at which point Charlie motored the skiff around and headed back to the *Zarina*.

"Charlie doesn't get to come to the hot springs with us?" Emilia gaped. I too was distraught at this idea. It seemed terribly unfair that with no place to dock, Charlie would be relegated to waiting on the *Zarina* while the rest of us sipped champagne (or juice, depending on the age appropriateness) and lounged in the hot springs.

"No, don't worry about Charlie," Karen said. "He'll take the skiff back to the *Zarina*, tie it up, and then come back to shore in the kayak." It was an elaborate means of getting a group of people and their belongings to shore in a place where it wasn't very easy to do so.

While Charlie made his way back and forth on various vessels, Karen, Mike, the girls, and I took in the layout of Goddard. A planked path led to a small structure not far from the beach, but we heard voices and saw backpacks nearby.

"It looks like that one's occupied," said Karen. "Let's head to the upper tub." She pointed a fair way up the hill in front of us, where the path continued up to another structure. Had I not known that the building housed a hot springs tub open to the public, I would never have ventured near. From a distance, the small wooden building looked like it might be home to a true mountain man. Someone who didn't like strangers and kept his rifle at the ready and ate small woodland creatures he snared in gruesome traps.

In light of the fact that Goddard was by no means an easy place to get to, I wondered what we would do if both hot springs were occupied. Jump right in and get cozy with strangers? Come back another time? A secret part of me hoped that was the case. Almost half of Alaska's thermal hot springs occur along the volcanic peninsula, and I imagined lava suddenly pouring into the bathing tub and cooking us all to death. I realize that there is no possibility of lava traveling through metal pipes to infiltrate a hot tub, but logic has never gotten in the way of me obsessing over improbable catastrophes. It is also possible that I spent too much of my youth watching absurd movies in which the characters experience just such a fate.

When we reached the open structure housing the second hot springs tub, we found we had it all to ourselves. A wooden roof and walls sheltered us from any rain that might come, but a large cutout window allowed open air and a view of the water. We hung our towels on a row of hooks and stripped our outer clothes down to the swimsuits we wore underneath.

"Awesome," said Ivy.

"I can't wait to get in," agreed Emilia.

The metal tub held brown tinted water. A million flecks of debris floated throughout. What were they comprised of? Skin cells of previous bathers? Would the experience be akin to marinating in the DNA of decades of previous hot tubbers? Two pipes fed into the structure from outside so that hot or cold water could be added as desired.

The children entered the steaming water. Karen and Mike followed.

"I can't believe how nice this is," said Mike. "It's so much better than what I remember growing up."

I sat on the edge and dipped in my feet. The color of the water brought to mind the image of that grizzled mountain man sitting naked in the tub, picking his teeth with a bone from a small animal.

"I know," agreed Karen. "It's so much better."

"What do you mean, Dad?" Emilia asked. "What was it like when you were growing up?"

"There wasn't a metal tub," Mike explained. "It was all wooden, and so sometimes the wood would feel . . ." He looked at me and trailed off. He could tell I struggled with the experience and didn't want to make it more off-putting than I already found it.

"Slimy," Karen chimed in. "Because it was wooden, it used to feel slimy."

I often find myself in these situations. I'll be in an exotic location doing something most people don't get to do and then feel like a complete asshole for not being more grateful for the experience, which I wrestle with because I'm too preoccupied worrying about mountain-man cooties.

Charlie joined us and slipped into the water with the others.

"Aren't you going to come in the water, Mom?" Ivy asked.

"Yes, I just have to get used to it," I said. This was true. It wasn't just the thought of cooties (which by this point I was sure I could feel nesting in between my toes) that kept me prudishly perched at the edge. I'm a temperature wimp as well. I've never understood others' ability to get right into a hot tub. To me it feels as if it's actually burning my skin, hence my fear of lava, and I take a painfully long time easing my way into the water.

"Can I have my snack?" Emilia asked.

"Yes," I answered.

"And let's go ahead and open the champagne," Karen suggested.

"Yes!" I agreed.

Over the years, I've learned that champagne is a proven remedy for my squeamish character. After two glasses, I finally got in the water.

We survived the hot springs with no molestation by bears, lava, cooties, or mountain men. When we were thoroughly pruned, Charlie headed back down to the kayak, paddled out to the *Zarina*, switched the kayak for the skiff, and motored back to get us.

"Thanks for the elaborate water taxi system," I said.

"No problem."

That night we anchored in a quiet cove and dined on shrimp, rice, and a salad, with ice cream for dessert. It was the sort of meal I would pay for heavily in a restaurant, and I marveled at Charlie and Karen's ability to pull it off from the confines of the *Zarina's* galley.

We played dominoes that evening, and I was dismayed to realize that I'm actually not smart enough to grasp the rules of Mexican train. The game was filled with alternating comments of, "Don't worry, this game is so easy," and "No, Amanda, you can't put that there."

As the evening faded into night, we readied for bed. The girls donned their pajamas, brushed their teeth, and crawled into the lower bunk. Charlie and Karen retired to the master while Mike and I slept in the salon. The table at which we'd eaten dinner and played dominoes transformed into our bed, and we slept soundly through the night.

The next morning, we motored to Maid Island, where we planned on picnicking later in the day.

"I was thinking we could try to fish on our way over there, but it looks like it's going to be too rough," Charlie informed us.

As he navigated through rough seas, Karen prepped sourdough pancakes and bacon for breakfast. She'd spent enough of her life on boats that she was adept at the culinary arts while the floor beneath her titled sharply.

Maid Island offered solid ground and sandy beach. We hauled our cooler ashore, packed with drinks and the makings of hot dogs we'd cook over a fire. We scavenged for dry wood and got a fair-sized bonfire going, all the while hoping to discover glass balls washed ashore. The glass balls are large Japanese fishing floats, no longer in use in the fishing industry but a popular find for beachcombers. The glass is often blue or green in tint, and they make wonderful decorative accents.

"You'll also want to keep your eye out for rubber duckies," Karen said.

"What?" I was sure I'd heard her wrong.

"In the early nineties, a cargo ship container got dumped into the sea. It was supposed to transport twenty-eight thousand rubber ducks from China to the United States. We still find them on beaches sometimes."

"You mean like a rubber ducky, like the bath toy?" Mike asked.

"Yes," she confirmed. "They're kind of like a collector's item."

"Hey, Mom." Emilia tugged at my jacket. "I have to go to the bathroom."

"Okay," I said. "You just have to pee?"

She looked at me silently.

"Oh. Okay, let me just get some . . . supplies." I gathered up toilet paper and plastic bags and envisioned digging a latrine with a stick. "Come on, girls. Come with me."

"But I don't have to go," Ivy protested, then reconsidered. "Well, I guess I'll try."

We trudged into the woods a ways, and I wondered what I'd do if we encountered a bear. I knew all of the things people were supposed to do when confronted by bears, but that isn't to say I'd remember them during the stress of such a situation. It was possible I'd keep my cool and react appropriately but also possible I'd throw the roll of toilet paper at the bear's head.

"I changed my mind, Mom," Emilia said. "I don't have to go." I'm not sure how one can have to poop one minute and then change their mind about it the next, but that's what Emilia did. She returned to the campfire. By this time, Ivy no longer protested and decided she had to go after all, the sudden urgency of which took precedence over my intention of digging a hole with a stick. It was a less than ideal affair and ended up with me returning to camp with a bag for later disposal.

"What is that?" Mike asked when we returned.

"You don't want to know."

"Why didn't you just bury it?"

"It just didn't work out that way. There was toilet paper involved, and it was . . . stuck, and I couldn't leave it there, and I ended up just sort of scooping up . . . stuff."

Mike looked at me blankly.

"Like scooping dog poop," I tried to explain. "Only more substantial. Well, depending on what size dog we're using for comparison."

"Tell me again, why you didn't just bury it?" he asked.

"I can't litter," I said. "Pack it in, pack it out. And I won't be responsible for burning down this island."

"What are you talking about?"

"You know, the poop fires."

The year prior in Boise, a biker in the hills had stopped to relieve himself. Not wanting to litter by leaving toilet paper behind, he attempted to light the toilet paper on fire. While this did destroy the toilet paper, it also started what would blossom into a seventy-three-acre wildfire. The story of the pooping cyclist made national headlines, and I felt the Bureau of Land Management did the right thing by not releasing the cyclist's name, instead limiting any identifiers to "the cyclist who had to relieve himself." The event wasn't at all relatable to our situation, as there was no chance of a wildfire occurring in our present climate.

"I'm hungry," Emilia announced.

"Right. Let me just take a quick hand sanitizer bath."

"Hey, Mom," said Emilia. "What do you use before you eat a meal on Christmas Eve?"

"I don't know. What?"

"Hand Santa-tizer. Get it?"

"Yeah, that's really . . . that's something."

We spent the afternoon roasting hot dogs over the fire and enjoying the serenity of the secluded beach. It was too chilly to remove our jackets or play in the water, but the scenery and company were lovely.

On our way back to Sitka that afternoon, we listened to Coast Guard reports of a boat adrift or possibly in distress. I hoped to hear a resolution and any mention of the fate of the entangled whale, but no other information came. The *Zarina* rocked wildly, and the girls again took Dramamine, sleeping for the duration of the return trip. As we braced ourselves in the salon and galley, I peeked down every few minutes at our sleeping children.

"They're not going to fly out of their beds, are they?" I asked Mike. The boat pitched at such an incline that I wasn't sure how they'd stayed put thus far.

"Let's hope not," he said.

I focused on keeping my stomach calm. I'm not prone to seasickness, and I could handle the motion of the boat pitching forward and then rising up, but adding in the side-to-side lurch took it to a new level. Were we going to be okay? I looked to the sky, expecting dark clouds webbed with lightning to come rolling overhead. Mike had no expression of worry, though he held on tightly to keep from being thrown about. Charlie focused intently on navigating the boat. I looked over to Karen, half-expecting her to be gathering up survival suits for everyone to wear. She stood with one hand on the galley counter to steady herself. With her other hand, she casually checked her phone.

"It's pretty amazing where you've lived," I said.

Karen looked up from her phone and smiled. "You mean on the boat?"

"Well, yes, living on a boat is amazing. But not just that. Living on Bamdoroshni Island and raising your kids there. Then moving to Mexico and having a home there and coming back here in the summer to live on the *Zarina*. I mean, it's all pretty amazing."

"It is," she agreed. "It's definitely not what most people are used to. And you know," she looked thoughtful for a moment, considering Alaskan island life, their home in Mexico, and living aboard the *Zarina*, "we haven't been able to flush toilet paper in forty years."

* * *

Russian Girl

It wasn't love at first sight. It took a full five minutes.

—Lucille Ball

My first experience on rough seas was at the age of twenty. Charlie was my captain. This was after I'd completed a study abroad program for a semester of my junior year in college. While in Moscow, I'd become close friends with Melissa, who later invited me to Alaska.

"My dad's a commercial fisherman. We can work on his boat, and you'll make enough money to cover your plane ticket," Melissa suggested.

I was already hooked on travel, and Alaska sounded adventurous. I'm not sure what I pictured when she said we could work on her dad's boat. She'd used the words "commercial fisherman," but I didn't have any clear image of what that was. This was long before reality television, and there was nothing along the lines of *Deadliest Catch* to either scare me away or spur me on. Up to that point in my life, the idea of fishing conjured up images of standing lakeside with a fishing pole and a cup of worms at my feet, or middle-aged men in a lazy boat on calm water, drinking beer and chatting under hats speckled with fishing lures. I had no idea what commercial fishing at sea would entail.

Having lived in Russia for four months, I had no trepidation about traveling alone, and I flew to Alaska on a series of flights zigzagging across the United States and finally delivering me to Sitka, where Melissa and her parents met me at the airport. They took me to their home on Bamdoroshni Island, the home Charlie and Karen have since sold to Dylan and in which he now lives with Ashley and his children. I was intrigued by Alaska, Alaskans, and the very idea of living on an island, something I'd always pictured made more sense in tropical climates. I couldn't fathom doing so in a northern setting. As amazing as I thought their island life was, I don't think I gained a true appreciation for it until after I had children. Karen and Charlie raising two children on the island, as Ashley and Dylan began doing thirty years later, was in my mind an incredible undertaking. I picture the handful of middle-of-the-night emergency room visits with my daughters in infancy and toddlerhood. Whenever that happened, it seemed like such a crisis, and we had to spring into action, driving the two blocks from our home in Boise to the emergency room. I couldn't fathom the stress of crossing the island on wet planks in darkness, making the journey via boat to town, and *then* driving to the emergency room. On the other hand, I had many middle-of-the-night trips to the emergency room with Ivy in Mexico, attempting to communicate in a mix of Spanglish and sign language, and I'm sure many parents can't fathom that experience. But our Mexico trip during Ivy's infancy was three months long. Charlie and Karen raised their children on the island for eighteen years.

"What was growing up here like?" I asked Melissa. "I mean, that's just so cool, growing up on an island."

"I hated it," she said.

Of course, I knew this. We'd had many late nights staying up talking in one of our dorm rooms in Moscow, drinking vodka and chatting the night away. She'd grown up with a faint sense of imprisonment, pining for the day when she could go off to college.

"What did Dylan think of it?" I asked.

"He loved it," she said. And this would be driven home when he'd purchase the island home from his parents years later.

When they welcomed me and we settled in, Melissa told me of our impending work. "So we'll start baiting tomorrow morning," she said. "And we'll be long-lining for black cod."

"Okay," I said, as if I had any idea what that meant.

Fishing was extreme in every sense—more difficult than anything I'd ever done but also more rewarding. It exhausted me every day, but I was energized by the experience at the same time. Before setting out, we spent two days baiting long lines with periodic hooks on them. The baiting process involved placing frozen squid on the hooks, then coiling the lines in three small circles, each partially overlapping the prior circle, until the fully baited line resembled a beach ball-sized coil of line. The job became harder as the squid thawed throughout the day, taking on a sickly sweet smell as they warmed in the sun and growing slippery and difficult to handle.

I became well acquainted with proper rain gear during

this time. Before then, I would have thought of rain gear as a rain jacket and perhaps some rubber boots. But fishing in Alaska requires serious attire. It's not just rain gear, it's "foul weather" gear. I borrowed gear from Karen since, as luck would have it, I was relatively the same size, boots included. The boots, thick rain pants, and heavy rain jacket go over your regular clothes, giving you the feeling of impenetrability, or at least the assurance that if someone threw a bucket of water at you, your underwear would stay dry. The outerwear isn't just to protect the wearer from rain or a splash of seawater or a random bucket from a water-wielding marauder but also to keep out the insidious fish scales that work their way onto every surface and into every crevice imaginable during the course of fishing. The scales act as a fish's final retaliation and protest at having been violently and rudely plucked from the sea.

When the baiting was done and the true fishing began, Charlie, Melissa, Dylan, and I set out. Our days at sea were long and took us to waters with no land in sight. We worked until our muscles ached and then beyond, falling into the ship's bunks at night with a fatigue I'd never known possible. It was both grueling and enjoyable, setting out the lines and returning to them a day later to haul in our catch.

As we let the lines out, I was prohibited from going near the back of the boat. This precaution, due to my inexperience, was to avoid having a flying hook catch me as the lines flew by. I was okay with this, as being hooked and dragged to the bottom of the sea wasn't high on my list. When we'd haul the lines back in, Charlie would snag the fish with a great gaff hook and throw them aboard, where Melissa and I would wrangle them and throw them down in the icy hold to Dylan, who not only packed the fish but also gave them a beating to the head if they were still moving.

We caught more than black cod on that trip, and I was endlessly amazed by the variety of creatures that would get snagged on one of the hooks and pulled onto the boat. Charlie often let me examine them before throwing them back. Sometimes these were other varieties of fish.

"What happens if we get a big crab or something tangled up in the line?" I asked.

"Then we eat good tonight," he said. "Oh, look, here's a . . ."

"A crab?" I asked hopefully.

"No," Charlie answered. "An asshole."

Of all the things he might have said, this was not an answer I anticipated.

"Why are they called assholes?" I asked. Stupidly.

"You'll see," said Melissa.

Charlie placed an object the size of an orange into my gloved hand. I looked to find an anemone-like creature with a single orifice surrounded by puckered flesh. "Oh." I nodded. "That's why."

I threw the asshole back into the sea, also not something I'd foreseen.

When the weeklong black cod expedition came to an end, I felt both exhausted and strong, and I knew that I'd only had a minor glimpse of what true fishermen undertake for an entire season, for a lifetime.

We returned to Sitka, and I took a shower and scrubbed myself raw. I was sure I'd never get all the scales from my hair or the scent of rotting squid from my nostrils. I cleaned up as best I could, and Melissa informed me of the rest of our plans for my remaining two days in Sitka before I'd fly back to Baltimore.

"Tomorrow we're going to get massages. It's always a nice treat after fishing. The woman who will do the massages is really good friends with my parents, so tomorrow night, she and her husband are having us all over for dinner and a bonfire."

"Okay," I said. "That sounds great."

I hadn't had a massage before, but I was still so exhausted the next day that I had no energy to spare on apprehension. The massage was wonderful, and only at one time did I wake myself with a loud snort.

"That was great," I told the masseuse when it was done. "Thank you so much."

"You're very welcome," she said. "And we'll see you this evening."

"Right, see you this evening."

That evening at the masseuse's house, I thanked her again and met her husband. They were a short, spunky couple and great fun to hang out with. Before long, I was doing tequila shots with them in their kitchen. The group laughed, ate, and drank, hanging around a bonfire. Occasionally, Melissa and I reverted to speaking in Russian. It was something unique we shared, and I'd felt my language skills slipping since returning from Moscow.

"Oh, hey, son," said our host. She greeted two young men, one of whom was her son, who had stopped by to say hello. Brief introductions were made, though conversation didn't extend much beyond "hello" and "nice to meet you" before the two guys said farewell and went on their way. In hindsight, it seems fated. The two guys would eventually become my husband and Melissa's husband. And our hosts, with whom

I'd thrown back shots of tequila, would become my in-laws. Years later, Mike and I spoke of that first meeting. "I remember it," I said. "It was just so brief. It was just like hello and goodbye."

"I probably would have talked to you more," said Mike, "but I thought you were some Russian girl. I didn't really know if you could speak English."

"What made you think that?"

"Because you were introduced to me as 'Melissa's friend from Russia.' So I thought you were Russian, and I also thought I heard you and Melissa speaking in Russian."

"Right," I said. "I can see how that would be confusing."

* * *

Theft of Daylight

Tlingit is pronounced "TLIN-git" or "KLIN-kit." This is an English pronunciation of their native word Lingit, *which means "people."*

—NativeLanguages.com

"Do you guys want to be park rangers?" I asked.

"Yeah," Emilia and Ivy cheered in unison.

"It's a big responsibility," Mike warned.

"Dad, I know we can do it," said Emilia. "Besides, you know how much I love birds. I will protect this park with my life."

"Maybe we should have some bear spray with us," Ivy said.

Sitka National Historical Park offers a Junior Ranger program and accompanying activity booklet. I was excited about this, not just because I want my children to be nature lovers as well as book nerds but also because the activity booklet represented something new with which to occupy the girls when we were out on the island and huddled indoors to stay out of the rain.

The activity book was as educational for me as it was for my children. It detailed information about caring for the planet, including how long it takes for everyday items to decompose (1+ million years for a Styrofoam cup). There were puzzles too hard for me, not having grown up with words like "devil's club" and "limpet" in my vocabulary. Incidentally, devil's club is a plant with ferociously irritating spines and not one to be trifled with. A limpet is an aquatic snail with a conical shell (as opposed to the coiled shell associated with a garden snail). If you have to take on either the devil's club or limpets, go for the limpets.

We learned about skunk cabbage, goosetongue, and chocolate lilies, which unfortunately smell like manure. Ivy was tasked with observing nature and reported that she heard "rain and eagles," smelled "ocean and leaves," and felt "happy and hot."

The activity book also included a Tlingit story about a boy trying to snare seagulls. When he says he's hungry, his mother gives him "the bony shoulder piece of a dried salmon with mold on the end." The boy is less than thrilled with this and throws it into the water. Then, in the course of trying to snare a seagull, he gets pulled under the water and spends a few years with the Salmon People. Then the Salmon Boy is swimming one day, and his father spears him, but just before his mother tries to cut him open to eat him, she sees her son's necklace. The Salmon Boy turns back into a real boy and tells his parents of his story.

The point of the story seems to be that you shouldn't complain about the food you are given, even if it happens to be moldy fish. But I'm left with so many other questions. If one did snare a seagull, how would one prepare it? Do fish really have shoulders? I find that more perplexing than the human-to-salmon-to-human transformation. And lastly, how long can I expect my children to have nightmares because they're traumatized by the idea of their dad spearing them and then me trying to cut them open and eat them for dinner? The activity book didn't answer any of these questions, but it did pose two questions of its own: 1. How did this story make you feel? 2. What did you learn from this story? My daughters completed almost every page in the activity book. This page remains blank.

Another Tlingit tale is the *Theft of Daylight*. This one also includes transformations and tells the tale of how Raven's trickery eventually led to the sun in the sky. The variations on the story, depending on the source, are vast, and it's an interesting example of how story and language and culture can change over time. *Theft of Daylight* is a creation story, and in it, Raven turns himself into a piece of dirt or hemlock needle (depending on which version you read) and drops himself into a cup of water. The water is consumed by a girl who becomes pregnant with Raven, who is then birthed in human form. This was all part of Raven's plan, and in baby form, he becomes annoying enough that his grandfather gives him the stars, moon, and sun to play with. Raven turns back into Raven, makes off with the celestial bodies, and brings them to the world as we know it.

I didn't share this story with my daughters because I could imagine them being afraid that they might not be themselves and that one day they would turn into birds and fly away. I was also concerned that they might ever after be nervous to drink water for fear of getting pregnant.

When the girls had completed the required number of pages in their activity books, it was time to do a service project. They were tasked with picking up five pieces of litter and disposing of them. We did this on the rocky beach in front of the visitor center.

"Hey, I found a shoe!" said Ivy.

"Does a dead crab count?" Emilia asked.

"No," I answered. "That dead crab is right where it's supposed to be."

"Yeah," she agreed. "I guess that's just nature. Do you want it, Mom?" She held up by one leg a crab the size of a drink coaster. The body of the crab had been punctured and the innards consumed. "I know how much you like crab."

"Tempting, but no thanks."

"Does this count as litter?" Ivy held up a giant section of foam, likely from a battered buoy.

"Oh yeah. That definitely counts," said Mike. "Good job, Ivy."

"Aw, man," Emilia pouted. "Ivy has more trash than me."

"Of all the things you think your kids might complain about, that one never crossed my mind," I said to Mike.

"Keep looking, Emilia," he instructed. "I guarantee you that you'll find plenty." There was no shortage of litter, most of it unidentifiable pieces of plastic having washed up on shore.

With the service project completed, we went inside the visitor center, where the girls presented their activity books to Ranger Mariah.

"Are you ready to be sworn in, then?" she asked.

"Yes!" Emilia snapped to attention in military fashion. Ivy eyed the plastic ranger badges in Ranger Mariah's hand.

In a quick ceremony, Ivy and Emilia dutifully repeated a

pledge and became National Park Service Junior Rangers. A popular part of Sitka National Historical Park is Totem Trail. Seeing a totem pole up close, which we did both inside the visitor center in Totem Hall as well as along the trail, is inspiring and intimidating. It has to be a terribly slow and painstaking process to carve one. And the pressure of knowing that you were creating something to communicate both your family's lineage and your culture's heritage would be overwhelming. Totems display incredible symmetry, and I imagined myself attempting to work on such a massive piece of art and then accidentally lopping off the ear of a wolf. Such things are sure to have happened. When I looked into the matter, I learned that the bottom ten feet of a totem pole are typically carved by a chief carver, and apprentices are permitted to work on the upper sections. This ensures that the portion of the pole that will be closest to the viewer and available for up-close observation is also the portion that is carved by an expert. The work of apprentices remains higher and further from view. This means that we've all been using the term "low man on the totem pole" incorrectly. It's actually a position of great importance.[8]

We wandered along Totem Trail admiring the impressive poles, and what had been a light mist turned to a steady drizzle.

"Do you guys want to head back now?" I asked.

"It's just rain, Mom," Ivy said.

"There's a spot up here that commemorates the battle between the Tlingit and the Russians," Mike said.

We made our way into an open field, what is known as "the fort site." It's the area where a Tlingit fort was thought to stand and where the battle of 1804, a bloody mark in the long, contentious relationship between Russians and Tlingits, likely occurred.

"Wait, there was a battle here?" Emilia asked.

"Yes," Mike confirmed.

Ivy toed the spongy ground. "Are there bodies buried here?"

"No," Mike said. "There aren't any bodies buried here."

I thought about telling them that even if bodies had been buried there, they would have long since decomposed, given the climate and the passage of over two hundred years, but I bit my tongue. This is one of many instances in my now decade of motherhood when I stopped myself from bringing up something morbid like decomposition, even though I'm endlessly fascinated by such topics.

"It's really starting to rain," I said. "Maybe we should head back to the truck." This time I was met with less resistance, and as we made our way back to the parking lot, I took note of the bumper stickers. There is one bumper sticker that can be seen more than any other in town. *FRIENDS DON'T LET FRIENDS EAT FARMED FISH: SUPPORT ALASKA'S WILD FISHERIES.*

I'd been associated with Alaskans and commercial fishermen long enough to have this phrase drilled into me. And it's no wonder that Alaskans are so passionate about fish when so much of their economy is tied to the fishing industry.

We climbed into the truck just as the rain stopped, and Mike suggested we visit the Sitka Sound Science Center, not far from the Sheldon Jackson Museum.

"I love science centers," Emilia declared.

"Do they have snacks there?" Ivy asked.

"I'm not sure, Ivy," Mike answered.

As it turned out, we arrived just as the center was closing for the day, but we could still walk along the adjacent Sheldon Jackson Hatchery area where the salmon were spawning.

The hatchery trains professionals in the world of aquaculture but also works in conjunction with Alaska's fisheries and the Alaska Department of Fish and Game to raise and release salmon. This helps maintain healthy fish populations. All of which is well and good but didn't change the fact that watching fish spawn made me feel a little bit like a voyeur. It's the same awkward feeling I get when walking a dog that needs to stop and poop. I'm compelled to give the creature a measure of privacy.

Emilia felt no such apprehension and peered intently at the fish.

"Are you looking at something in particular, Emilia?" I asked.

"Just checking on the fish," she said, then tapped her National Park Service Junior Ranger badge. "Just doing my job."

* * *

Fortress of the Bear

What on earth would I do if four bears came into my camp?
Why, I would die of course. Literally shit myself lifeless.

—Bill Bryson, *A Walk in the Woods*

Though we had many adventures in town and on the water, we had equal hours holed up on the island, hoping for the rain to end. Mike went through periods inundated with work, and I did my best to be the primary parent, to allow him time to deal with clients back home. He does the same for me as the need arises. As such, the girls and I engaged in marathon games of Monopoly. It takes a measure of perseverance to do this. You must submit yourself to the interminable monotony of Monopoly and trust that the game will eventually, mercifully come to an end. Ivy won every game. I'm thinking of making her my financial advisor.

We were due for a break from ourselves by the time my in-laws came to town. They were coaches and physical education teachers for thirty-five years in Sitka before retiring to Mexico, where they live in the same town that Charlie and Karen live in when not on the *Zarina*. We were ecstatic to have a few days of travel overlap with them when they arrived near the end of our trip; Nana and Papa were a sight for bored eyes.

We had uncharacteristic sunshine when they arrived and decided to take advantage of it by visiting Fortress of the Bear, a nonprofit bear-rescue facility.

"I feel like I've been out here before," I said as we drove five miles from downtown Sitka along Sawmill Creek Road.

"You and I came out here when they first opened," my mother-in-law answered. "When Emilia was a baby."

"Wait, that creepy little petting zoo? *That's* where we're going?" I remembered nine years prior, on the same trip I'd dressed Emilia as a bear cub and dodged huge piles of scat, my mother-in-law had driven me out to an odd place that appeared to sit on the ruins of an old factory. It wasn't any sort of established attraction that was open to the public, and I recalled an assortment of ducks and pigs wandering about in a large concrete enclosure.

"Yes," my mother-in-law confirmed. "That's exactly where we're going."

I couldn't figure out why she was so enthusiastic about it or why we'd even return. And I regretted getting my girls excited about the visit, as it was sure to be a disappointment. I pictured malnourished bear cubs in tiny metal cages.

I could not have been more wrong.

Fortress of the Bear was an astounding facility with enormous enclosures for two sibling groups of brown bears and three black bears. Converted from an old pulp mill, the three large areas walled in concrete had long ago been used to store chemicals for dissolving wood pulp into eventual paper but now serve as bear habitats. Viewing platforms sit above the enclosures so that visitors can look down on the animals.

The bears were playful and active in habitats with ponds, flowing water, and salmon to catch. We met an intern named Sydney, who fiddled around with buckets.

"What are you doing?" Emilia asked.

"I'm getting ready to give the bears their Popsicles," she said. The buckets had been filled with fruit and then to the top with water before being frozen. Sydney removed the frozen blocks of fruit from the buckets and chucked them down into the water in the bear enclosures. Some of the bears played with their treats for a bit, while others settled right into eating.

"This place is absolutely amazing," I said. I was leaning on a railing looking down into the enclosure, where two bears halfheartedly wrestled. I looked to my left and realized that the man standing next to me was one of the founders, the same man who had given my mother-in-law and me a private tour of the grounds after he'd first acquired them. I vaguely remembered him trying to communicate his vision for the place back then and chided myself for not giving him more credit and instead writing off the place as a "creepy little petting zoo."

The orphaned bears at Fortress of the Bear will stay there for the duration of their lives, because they've been raised from cubs and have no ability to care for themselves in the wild. How would they make their own Popsicles? But the eventual goal of the place is to create a rehabilitation program so that orphaned bears can be released back into the wild. As it is, orphaned cubs are often shot by the Department of Fish and Game because they have no alternative course of action.

This seems tragic, but if there is no registered request for a cub from a zoo or other suitable facility, that's the outcome. I watched the bears playing and thought they had a pretty good life, given the alternative.

"So what's the scariest thing that's ever happened here?" The questioner was a middle-aged woman from another group.

The founder turned to her and said, "The scariest thing? That's easy. It was when they were cubs and broke through the ice and I almost couldn't get them out. I thought two of them were going to drown. That was definitely the scariest thing."

I could tell the woman wasn't satisfied with this answer. She'd been hoping for a story of a bear on the verge of escape or of a tourist falling into the enclosure, a scenario in which human life was at stake. Her natural inclination to morbidity made me wonder if we were related.

"Hey, what's that?" Ivy asked.

Sydney the intern and I followed her gaze to the shallow water below.

"That's part of a walker," Sydney explained. "There was someone here yesterday whose walker fell in. You can see the other parts of it over there."

I began to identify various parts of the walker.

"How on earth did someone's walker fall in?" I asked.

I saw the potential for a dropped phone or camera, as we could lean over the rail and take unobstructed pictures of the beasts, but I could see no way in which a walker could be easily lost over the edge.

"I have no idea," Sydney admitted.

"It looks like the bears had fun with it," I commented, noting the complete destruction of the walker and the distance over which it was scattered. A breezeway connected two of the bear habitats, and I imagined part of Sydney's job was to clean the bear enclosure when all of the animals were barricaded in on the other side. In addition to what must be an enormous amount of bear poop to scoop, Sydney would have to gather the remnants of the walker.

The woman who'd asked about the owner's scariest moments scanned the habitat furiously. I assume she was searching for senior citizen body parts or a tuft of white hair, perhaps a hearing aid, in the event that the walker's owner had gone over the edge as well. After a minute, she resigned herself to no such find.

In twenty years of knowing my husband, my in-laws, and a host of other Alaskans, I've heard my share of bear stories. These are often dramatic encounters that occurred while the storyteller was deer hunting, stories of guns misfiring, bears felled at the last moment of a full charge, coming to rest within feet of would-be victims. There are tales of bears stalking humans, poaching hunters' kills, and charging up steep inclines with frightening speed.

I also learned of bear horror stories through Corinne, a friend who lives in Seward, on the Kenai Peninsula. Seward was home to Alaskan flag designer Benny Benson, is the site of Mile 0 of the historic Iditarod Trail, and holds an annual Polar Bear Jump-Off to raise money for the American Cancer Society, because people love to watch other people in painful situations, like jumping into frigid waters while wearing costumes. But Seward residents also contend with bear encounters, and Corinne periodically e-mails me with details. These aren't the typical run-ins with which Alaskans are familiar, like hikers surprising bears along trails, but rather increasingly bold bears, raiding her backyard chicken coop, coming onto her porch. One such bear was shot, and the neighborhood came together the following day for a bear-skinning party. I've never been invited to, nor attended, a bear-skinning party, but I'm pretty sure it's a lot like when neighbors on our Boise street get together and order pizza.

Corinne went so far as to e-mail me a picture of the skinned bear head. I'm sure this was to show the size of the animal's teeth, but never having seen a freshly skinned anything before, the jaws were the least shocking part. Corinne and her neighbors didn't relish the bear's death but did feel relief at the abatement of a significant threat. And while the only way I can fathom the gruesomeness of a bear-skinning party is to joke about it, I'm sure skinning a bear and harvesting the meat for stew (nothing goes to waste) is incredibly hard work. Isn't there a saying about skinning bears? Something about it taking a village? Oh wait, that's child rearing.

While I prefer the bears at Fortress of the Bear, Corinne's experiences are also an unfortunate reality.

"Look, Mom. Ducks!" Ivy pointed to a pair of ducks paddling lazily about in one of the ponds. The bears and ducks showed no interest or concern for one another.

"And there are eagles here, too," Emilia added. She pointed out two bald eagles in the nearby trees. An immature eagle (thus identified not because it was obnoxious but due to its mottled brown color as opposed to the more familiar white-feathered head of a mature eagle) landed on the rim of the concrete fifteen feet from us. We'd been close to plenty of eagles in zoos and raptor centers, but this was an unprecedented encounter with a wild bird.

"I don't know where to look," I said to Mike.

"It's pretty hard not to watch the giant bears right in front of us."

"Agreed, but a raptor with a six-foot wingspan is sitting *right there.*"

"But one of the bears is now swimming across the pond."

"That's awesome," I acknowledged. The bear looked to be enjoying itself. With just its head gliding above the surface of the water, and from the right angle, I could almost convince myself it was a giant Labrador. "But the eagle is now looking right at me."

The curve of an eagle's beak gives it the appearance of frowning. The eyes, too, seem severe and serious, and the overall impression is of a mildly annoyed bird in a constant state of focus. But this is just the result of trying to read human expression from a beaked, feathered head, which you can't really do. Maybe the bird was happy. Perhaps it was giving me the equivalent of a bird smile and it wanted to perch on my arm and let me pet it. Surely that was why it stared so intently. Or maybe it wanted to bite off my earlobe. I'm certain it was one of the two.

We stared at each other for a full five minutes. I wanted to name it, and wavered between Poppet or Death Feather. Likewise, it was probably deciding whether to think of me as Mama or Big Meat Snack.

When the eagle flew away, disappointingly without perching on my arm or removing one of my earlobes, we bade farewell to the bears as well. Walking back to the parking lot, my mother-in-law said, "I wonder if there is anyone here who would want to go out for ice cream?"

Emilia and Ivy showered her with shouts of "Me! Me!" and jumped up and down.

"Oh," she said in mock surprise. "You do? Well, I guess we better do that then. Is there any place in particular we should go?"

"Let's go to the brewery," Emilia suggested.

"Yes," Ivy echoed. "Can we please go to the brewery?"

"Well, that's not what I expected to hear, but I guess so," she said.

Sitka's Baranof Brewery offered, in addition to a variety of beer, excellent root beer floats, and we'd taken the girls there on a handful of occasions when making trips into town.

We settled in at the brewery, the girls fawning over their root beer floats and the adults sipping a flight of beer. The room had a fair amount of heads mounted on the walls, not atypical décor in Sitka.

"Oh, wow," said my father-in-law, looking up. I followed his gaze to the head of a mountain goat. "I shot that goat."

It never occurred to me that a hunter could recognize his kill from decades prior, like a painter might recognize a piece of their art.

I almost said, "That's awful." But hunting is a normal part of life in Alaska and often occurs for subsistence rather than sport. My father-in-law hunted for the duration of his years in Sitka, as filling the freezer from a successful hunt (as well as harvesting what he could from the sea) was far more economical for feeding his family than using their teachers' salaries to buy overpriced meat shipped up from the Lower 48.

My father-in-law surprised me then by adding, "I'll never forget it. It was awful."

"What do you mean?" I asked.

"The shot didn't kill it," he explained. "It was terrible. So many people think hunting is shooting an animal and it dies.

That's not always the case. I remember that goat because I had to slit its throat. It was awful and messy and not fast and really horrific."

"Oh," I said. "That is awful. How did it end up here?"

"I'm not sure," he said. "When we left, I ended up donating a lot to various places."

I looked up at the goat and tried to think of a bright side.

"Well," I said, "a brewery isn't the worst of final resting places."

* * *

Porky, Bishop Innocent, and the Heckler

In death, you get upgraded into a saint no matter how much people hated you in life.

—Sarah Vowell

In the seventies, a five-foot-two legendary logger who went by Porky ignited one hundred tires in Mount Edgecumbe's crater to convince Sitkans that the volcano was erupting. This was an April Fools' Day prank that the culprit spent four years planning. This story disturbs me on several levels, not the least of which is that anyone would go by the name "Porky." And who spends four years planning an April Fools' Day prank? But the worst of it is that he would lead others to think a volcano was about to erupt—and think that was funny. There's nothing funny about Pompeii. I wondered if, when Mount St. Helens erupted six years after Porky's prank, he still found it funny.

My in-laws, who lived in Sitka at the time, attest that

Porky's prank hadn't resulted in panicked people running about in chaos. "I don't think any of us actually believed it was erupting. The reaction was more like, 'Wow, how'd he pull off that one?'" my mother-in-law assured me. The answer to that question involves a helicopter to get the tires into the crater and dynamite to ignite them.

"And of course he never took the tires back out," my father-in-law added.

"So they're still there?" I asked.

"What's left of them. State officials were not happy. I think they wanted to prosecute him, but they couldn't for some reason."

The impression I got was that Sitkans were tolerant and good-natured when it came to Porky and his pranks. One notable exception to this was when Porky hired "ladies of the evening," as my mother-in-law described them, to come from Juneau during Sitka's annual Fourth of July parade. They rode on a parade float with Porky and, upon reaching the steps of the post office in the center of town, removed their shirts. I don't know if this constitutes a prank; it sounds more like an inappropriate expression of Porky's love for boobs. In any case, not all Sitkans were amused, chief among them Porky's wife.

"She almost killed him," my father-in-law said.

"The streets were packed with all of these families out to watch the parade, so it didn't go over well. He went to jail for that one," my mother-in-law added. "But the Mt. Edgecumbe prank, that's the one that made him famous. Should we take the girls to the Russian Bishop's House?"

I marveled at how quickly the conversation could move from "ladies of the evening" to "the Russian Bishop's House."

"It's a really interesting attraction here in Sitka if the girls are into that sort of thing," she continued.

"Yeah, we love museums," I confirmed. "Let's check it out."

The Russian Bishop's House was built in 1843 as a residence for Bishop Innocent, who held considerable power in shaping the Orthodox Church in what was then known as Russian America. I wondered how difficult it would be to walk around with an identity like Bishop Innocent. It would seem like a terrible amount of pressure. Constantly living up to Innocent would strain any human, no matter how pious. Maybe that's why Porky was okay with being known as Porky. The name automatically lowers the bar.

Luckily for both Innocent and the people inhabiting the lands he influenced, he was known as a good guy, so much so that the Russian Orthodox Church declared him a saint almost a hundred years after his death. Part of why Innocent had the good-guy vibe was his interest in native cultures. Instead of trying to stamp out the indigenous languages, he learned them, and he wrote scholarly works in both Russian and Aleut.

Touring the Russian Bishop's House was an hour of trying to read interesting bits of information on placards while also struggling to keep up with Emilia and Ivy, who pinballed from one exhibit to the next with questions of "What's this?" (as if I can answer such a thing from across the room) and commands of "Look at this!" (but why bother crossing the room to look if by the time I get there you'll have moved and be back at "What's this?"). I like museums, and I like visiting them with my kids, but I was a nerd long before I ever became a parent, and I often lament that I can't take time to read about each exhibit and learn the information that I will retain almost until lunchtime.

We left the Russian Bishop's House and headed to a pub for lunch. I like the word pub because it implies a bar with a children's menu, so everyone is happy. The Bayview Pub had not only a bar and a children's menu but also darts, pool tables, and a large selection of board games. This made up for the logo, a fairly crude drawing of a woman holding a salmon in one hand and a beer in the other, sitting on a barrel and clad in a yellow hat and raincoat and a pair of the ubiquitous Xtratufs, the rubber boots of choice in Southeast Alaska. Maybe it's not a rain jacket but a dress, as it's smartly belted and shows cleavage flanked by bulbous breasts. If it is a raincoat, then the picture makes no sense because in reality she'd also have the matching yellow rain pants. In the logo, however, she doesn't have any pants and is in the process of crossing her legs. If the picture was a moving picture, it'd be just a second shy of flashing her genital area. I understand why they went with this picture. It really speaks to Alaskan culture, because I can't count how many times I ran into half-dressed, impossible-body-proportioned women sitting on barrels, holding fish and beer, during our trip. I mean, they're just everywhere.

That evening, we walked down to Old Harbor Books, where I was scheduled for a reading and book signing. Karen and Charlie were there, along with Melissa and Michael, my in-laws of course, and other friends and relatives.

"Thank you all for coming," I said. "I'm going to read a kid-friendly passage today." The small crowd giggled and glanced at Emilia and Ivy in the front row. I'd never had my daughters in attendance at a reading before, but by that point, they seemed old enough for it. So instead of reading my sometimes profanity-laced pieces, I'd specifically selected a G-rated passage. After the reading, I thanked everyone again for coming and asked if there were any questions. Emilia's hand shot up into the air.

"Um, yes, Emilia. You have a question?"

"Do you just write about us or do you also write about other people?" she asked.

"That's a very good question. Sometimes I'll write about the people we meet along the way, or the people we learn about," I thought of the stark contrast of the day's characters, from Porky to Bishop Innocent, "but most of what I write about involves our family and our adventures."

A few other people asked questions before Emilia's hand shot up again.

"Yes, Emilia?"

"When are you going to let your daughters read your books?"

The others laughed nervously. Part of this has to with the nature of my first series, which talks about the trials of parenting and some of my personal embarrassments, like that time I smoked pot and crapped my pants in the middle of a dinner party. (Hasn't everyone?) Then there are other things they might not be ready for, like just how often I write about them.

"I'm not sure, but I don't think you're ready for them quite yet," I said.

"But why not?" she demanded.

"Because most of what's in the books is meant for adult readers," I answered.

"So, when *will* I be allowed to read your books? I mean, I'm your daughter, so don't you think I should read them?"

"When you're older," I said.

"But why not now?"

"Some of my books have bad words in them that aren't appropriate for you to read."

"Well, why do you use bad words?" she countered.

Everyone else in the store sat back with arms folded and watched the show as Emilia hurled question after question at me, essentially heckling her own mother.

"Okay then," I said a little too loudly. "I guess we are just about out of time."

As I finished up the book signing, Emilia approached and whispered in my ear, "We're not done with this conversation, you know."

The bookstore closed for the evening as a large group of us, planning for a late dinner together, gathered on the sidewalk to coordinate.

"So, are we headed to the Angry Maid?" my father-in-law asked.

"You mean the Mean Queen?" I challenged.

"Oh, right. What did I say?"

"Yes, Dad," Mike said. "We're going to the Mean Queen."

But when we attempted to revisit my favorite Sitka restaurant, we found that it was too crowded to accommodate our numbers.

"Let's head back to the Bayview Pub," Mike suggested. "They had plenty of room there." I agreed; not only did they have room to accommodate us, but it had been a full four hours since the last time we'd taken our children to a bar.

"Mom, can we play this?" Ivy asked, pointing to the pool table as we settled in at the pub.

"I'm not sure, Ivy," I said. "Most of the time, these aren't for kids to play on."

"It's okay," said a nearby bartender. "As long as an adult is playing with them, we're fine with it."

"Well, let's see if another adult wants to play, too," I said. "We can play on teams."

"I'm on Mom's team," Ivy declared.

"Phyllis, do you want to play a game of pool with me and the girls?" I asked. Phyllis is a local artist and longtime family friend, and we hadn't seen much of her on the trip.

"Sure, I'd love to," she said.

We played until our food came, not making much progress with the game but appeasing the kids' desire to play nonetheless.

"Let's take a break," I said as the waiter delivered our meals.

Emilia and Ivy picked at their food, likely still full from our earlier visit and far more fixated on returning to the game.

"Are you done, Mom?" Ivy asked. "It's your turn."

"You have to give us a minute to eat, Ivy."

She counted to sixty and asked, "Are you done now?"

"I'll be there in just a second," I relented.

"We can't play yet," Emilia commanded. "We have to wait for Phillip!"

"Phyllis," I corrected. "Not Phillip."

"Oh, right. Sorry," Emilia said.

"That's okay." Phyllis smiled.

"Are you almost done, Phillip?" she asked.

"Phyllis, not Phillip," I corrected again.

"Got it," said Emilia.

Emilia and Ivy hadn't heard the name Phyllis before but were more than acquainted with the name Phillip, as Prince Phillip is a prominent character in Sleeping Beauty. Of course my daughters know the 1959 Disney movie, not the earlier versions of the story, which far predate the Brothers Grimm, going all the way back to the 1300s, and include themes like rape, suicide, and cannibalism—perfect stories from which to develop classic children's tales.

In addition to a familiarity with the name Phillip, but not Phyllis, Emilia and Ivy have no grasp of the typical genders associated with names. Our good friends Mark and Rachel come to visit periodically in Boise, and for two years straight, both Emilia and Ivy would say, "Okay, so Mark and Rachel are coming. And which one is the boy and which one is the girl?" Separating the two into their respective genders was exasperating to them, and they much preferred to think of the couple as a single unit known as MarkAndRachel.

Phyllis and I had a few minutes during the evening to catch up, and I learned that in addition to the pottery for which she is known as an artist, she'd been studying and experimenting with new media.

"I've been doing some really cool things with fish skin," she said, "learning how to manipulate it and incorporate it into art."

The first time I'd encountered the phrase "fish skin," at the Sheldon Jackson museum, I thought it not the most attractive marriage of words, maybe a step above "seal gut." But when I considered what Phyllis was doing, learning about native art and incorporating it into her own, it seemed a beautiful pursuit, a contrast of two Alaskan artistic expressions. It's the acknowledgment of those contrasts that exist in a place that truly makes it come alive for me. An image struck me: Bishop Innocent and Porky the practical joker sitting together at the pub, under the sexy, fish-wielding beer maid logo.

My thoughts were interrupted as Emilia turned to the table and loudly called, "Come on, Phillip, it's your turn."

* * *

Reunion

I was eating in a Chinese restaurant downtown. There was a dish called
Mother and Child Reunion. It's chicken and eggs. And I said,
"I gotta use that one."

—Paul Simon

By design, our trip to Sitka coincided with Mike's twentieth high school reunion. I've never been to a reunion of my own, as I always seem to be either out of the country or about to give birth when they occur. The giving birth hitch is behind me, but the chance of being out of the country remains.

The idea of my high school reunion brings an odd mix of emotions. There's curiosity about my classmates and what it would be like to reconnect. They've gone on to become jewelry designers, educators, NASA engineers, and end-of-life doulas. But there's also the fear that those same classmates might feel compelled to remind me what an asshole I was.

Mike didn't have this problem because, by all accounts, he was not an asshole.

The first night of the reunion weekend involved meeting

for drinks at the Channel Club. For some, the opening hour was mired in the awkwardness of classmates reuniting after two decades apart and spouses lurking on the fringe. Others in attendance still lived in Sitka, were acquainted with their fellow Sitkans' lives and families, and saw each other regularly in the course of small-town life. Whatever the degree of awkwardness, it melted away by the second hour of the evening, aided by the second round of drinks.

Our children, along with Michael and Melissa's children, were in the care of Michael's mother. A guest room awaited us in their home whenever we wanted to call it a night. With freedom from both the island and motherhood for the evening, I celebrated by consuming unhealthy amounts of alcohol at an unadvisable rate. Maybe it was the intoxication, but everyone I met seemed genuinely kind. Had there been not one asshole in my husband's graduating class? I felt as if I was constantly being introduced to my new best friend. I spoke with one such woman and gave her my phone number. She texted me on the spot so that we could keep in touch. When I read the message the following day, I couldn't remember which of my new best friends the message was from, so didn't respond at all. Still an asshole, after all these years.

We ended up at the Pioneer Bar, or P Bar, as it is known. It's an institution in Sitka, decorated in hundreds of framed photos dating back decades. Pictures of men with their boats, men with their catch, men with their fishing buddies, posed pictures and action shots, some of them harrowing. It's the bar where retired men meet in the mornings for coffee, hardcore drinkers get plastered at night, and commercial fishermen go after spending days or weeks at sea. The P Bar has legacy. None of this means that it's clean or pleasant. It's dark, dingy, and smells like a mix of fish, cigarettes, beer, and urine, but when you've gotten mildly liquored up in more elegant surroundings before venturing into the P Bar, you don't care.

The Channel Club and the P Bar were an oddly fitting combination of places to host a group of people who were born and raised in Sitka. At the Channel Club, you can dine on fresh fish and prime rib. At the P Bar, you can have all the secondhand smoke your lungs desire. Altogether, you have a decent representation of town.

After a few hours at the P Bar (or possibly twenty minutes), I let Mike know in clear terms that I'd reached the point of no longer being able to function as an adult human, and we stumbled back to Michael and Melissa's.

The schedule for the next day involved a kid-friendly picnic at "The Rec," a shoreline recreation area, which Mike had a hand in organizing.

"I'm afraid no one is going to show up," Mike said.

"What makes you say that?"

"I only had a few people respond to say they'd bring something. So either people aren't going to show, or they're going to show and we're not going to have enough food."

"Well, let's bring a bunch of food and drinks, just in case," I suggested.

"I'm going to order ten pizzas, and we'll bring a cooler full of drinks, too," he said.

We arrived at the picnic location with our cooler, towering stack of pizza boxes, and children in tow.

"Someone reserved this shelter just up ahead," Mike said, leading the way down a trail.

"It looks like someone went all out decorating it, too," I commented. I saw streamers and colorful tablecloths, but as we rounded to the front of the shelter, we saw that the streamers and tablecloths were not for us.

"Can we help you?" a woman asked me. She was flanked by fellow octogenarians on all sides, a white-haired army.

"We have this space reserved for a high school reunion," Mike explained.

"No, you don't," she said. "We have a party scheduled here."

"Oh. Okay then," Mike said weakly.

I'm not sure that it was ever determined who had properly reserved the space, but it didn't really matter. The elderly shindig was in full swing, and they made it clear they had no intention of relocating, even if we were to prove our reservation.

"What do you want to do?" I asked Mike.

"Well, I guess we'll just have to find another space."

"I agree. They looked ready to rumble if need be."

We moved to a nearby fire ring and set of picnic tables as other classmates began to trickle in. Emilia and Ivy quickly made friends as other children showed up, playing tag and exploring the forested area of towering trees and the rocky beach to which it gave way. We adults assessed our various hangover levels and chatted about the night before. After the P Bar, the diehards had continued on with an all-night bonfire.

"I woke up and didn't know where the hell I was," said a man named John. "My face was all smashed up against the ceiling." After John passed out, others somehow ratcheted him to the ceiling of a garage. Figuring out how to ratchet a human body to the ceiling of a garage must take a unique skill set. That's résumé worthy. John deserved recognition as well. It's hard enough to wake with a hangover. A splitting headache combined with the need to urinate and rehydrate is not a happy place to be. In addition to being unable to move, having no knowledge of where you are and no understanding of why gravity isn't working as it should must be downright terrifying.

Along with stories of the previous night, the former classmates relived high school memories. A guy named Tim recounted wearing his brand-new hunting gear, having to relieve himself, and accidentally crapping on the strap of his new overalls bib.

"All I could do was cut off the strap," he said. "And when I went back to the group with one strap cut off, they all just started laughing because they knew exactly what had happened."

"You grew up in a different world," I said to Mike. In high school, I didn't know anyone who hunted, owned camouflage overalls, or found themselves in situations that necessitated crapping outside. Teenagers went to the mall for fun and worked at retail shops and fast-food joints. Getting outdoors meant a long bike ride or feeding ducks at a pond. Sitkans grow up camping, hunting, boating, fishing, and sometimes crapping along the way. As well, they have pocketknives on them when it's necessary to cut away an article of clothing on which they've pooped.

"Well, I guess I didn't need to worry about no one showing up," said Mike. The group quickly grew to crowd the tables and mill about the fire. Children whooped and hollered with endless energy and a steady refrain of laughter.

"And I guess we didn't need to bring ten pizzas," I added. Not only did people show up, they brought their own giant coolers of drinks to share, homemade casseroles, baked treats, and a seafood feast. The pizza looked the least appetizing alongside halibut, shrimp, and clusters of crab legs. "These people really know how to picnic."

My in-laws had graciously offered (after we'd strongly suggested it multiple times) to watch Emilia and Ivy for the second evening of the reunion. That night, the group would meet for a last get-together at Totem Square Hotel, and Mike and I rented a room there to again save us a trip back to the island.

Like the previous evening, it began tamely enough with drinks and food. At ten o'clock, the restaurant staff informed us that they were closing.

"You can't close," someone said. "It's ten o'clock. We're having a high school reunion. That's why we booked this place."

"Oh," said a waiter. "Well, we're only open until ten."

Clearly there had been miscommunication when setting up the event (much like our wedding reception at the Raptor Center), and the reunion group grumbled and looked to one another, wondering where to go next. When the waiters returned, we anticipated them handing out bills and clearing drinks, but they brought the news that they'd called the boss, who agreed they could keep the place open if we kept drinking.

"I'm pretty sure that's not going to be a problem," someone said.

They kept the restaurant open for us and turned on music, and a dance floor formed. The guys in the group, including the overalls shitter and the one who woke that morning strapped to someone else's garage ceiling, began a contest of ridiculous dance moves. One of these involved lying down and humping the floor. This garnered substantial laughter, so other guys joined in, not wanting to be outdone. After executing the move, one guy stood up, turned to the man next to him, and asked, "What did I look like?" I'm not sure how his friend responded or what the dancer hoped to hear. "You looked great" or "Really cool"? Or was he looking for more constructive criticism. "Go lower in the hips, dude. Really try to think about your form."

With this unique form of entertainment, I overindulged for the second night in a row, again unfettered by responsibility. If memory serves correct, and there's a 62 percent chance that it does, I stopped short of humping the floor, so I'm calling it a win.

Attending Mike's reunion lessened my apprehensions about attending one of my own. No matter what the maturity level of classmates, then or now, the weekend made it clear that the intent was shared laughter and a general wish of goodwill for those with whom you spent your formative years. And I'm pretty sure none of my classmates will ratchet me to the ceiling.

* * *

Bathing with Strangers

The cool thing about being famous is traveling. I have always wanted to travel across seas, like to Canada and stuff.

—Britney Spears

"How did you like Alaska?" I asked the girls as we began our return trip on the Alaska Marine Highway.

"It was good," said Emilia casually, as if the Last Frontier was akin to a satisfying meal.

"Think of all the wildlife we saw on this trip," Mike said.

"We saw bears, sea lions, bald eagles, elk, and that rockfish that we cut open," said Ivy.

"I wish we'd seen whales, though," Emilia lamented. "That's the one thing we didn't get to see."

We stared out the ferry window in silence for a moment before watching a whale surface multiple times alongside the ferry.

"Oh my gosh!" Emilia shrieked. "Did you guys just see that?"

"I guess we can now cross whales off the list," I said.

When we'd left America to cross into Canada at the beginning of our adventure, we'd received little more than "Have a nice trip." This was despite all of my research and worry regarding the endless questions we'd face about what we were doing and what laws we might be breaking. When the ferry docked in Prince Rupert and we found ourselves reentering Canada, we had a much more wary customs official. Perhaps we looked less wholesome and more suspect after living on an island for a month. In any case, the officer posed a series of questions directly to Emilia, giving us a warning look that we'd best remain silent and not try to answer for her. Emilia did splendidly, answering him cheerfully and honestly, not once betraying us by talking about how much wine I drink or deciding to see what would happen if she suggested that she'd been kidnapped. I'm thankful for that.

Our travels back through Canada took us through a town called Houston.

"Hey, look," I said, motioning to a billboard. "Apparently this place is home to the world's largest fly rod."

"Well, I guess that's something to be proud of," said Mike.

"I almost feel like we should go see it," I said. "But more of me feels like not doing so."

We didn't see the rod in person, but I was compelled to look it up after the fact. The sixty-foot, eight-hundred-pound rod was the idea of a local while attending a tourism workshop. Maybe he thought Houston needed a monument to go along with its designation as "The Steelhead Capital of the World," and creating the world's largest fly rod seemed like a great fit. On the one hand, I'm surprised that this idea, which included hundreds of hours of donated labor from local businesses, reached fruition. In addition, shares of the fly rod were sold to raise money for its completion and installation. In fact, there are still shares available, and you can buy your very own piece of the rod by visiting the Houston Visitor Information Centre (where you can also see their stuffed grizzly, a 975-pound bear that stood eleven feet tall and poached local cattle).

On the other hand, I've met enough fanatical fishermen in my life to understand that, yes, there are plenty of people who would see this as a worthwhile endeavor. The fly rod is a permanent installation at Steelhead Park, where fly fishermen can stare at it adoringly, and the rest of us can wonder at what looks from a distance like a big stick poking up toward the sky.

After Houston, we drove through Vanderhoof, which we'd soon learn had its own claim to fame.

"Where are we now?" Mike asked.

"I think we're coming up on Vanderhoof. That's fun to say. Vander*hoof*!" This last time, I added a Norwegian accent.

"And that's exactly why we could never live here," said Mike.

"Because I'd be walking around saying 'Vanderhoof!' all the time?"

"Exactly."

When I first heard that Vanderhoof held an annual Wild Goose Chase, I was fraught with excitement. Until that moment, I'd never acknowledged my hidden desire to chase a wild goose. Could I actually catch one? What would I then do with it? How much would I traumatize the goose in the process? How much physical trauma would the goose cause me? I imagined the event taking place in an area frequented by wild geese. Participants would flounder about trying to catch a goose, and I'd win a shiny medal and substantial prize money when I'd be the first to catch one. After a photo op, I'd return my goose to its wild state.

Imagine my disappointment when I learned that the event isn't the Vanderhoof Annual Wild Goose Chase but the Vanderhoof Annual Wild Goose Chase Fun Run. You don't actually get to chase a goose.

"But look!" I said, pointing to Vanderhoof's billboard. "It's the geographical center of British Columbia."

"You're joking," Mike said. "Was there really a sign that said that?"

"I'm not making it up, I swear."

"We're in the center of the earth?" Emilia asked from the back. "Maybe we should stop and take a picture or something."

"Actually," Mike agreed, "that's not a bad idea."

"You really want a picture of the geographical center of British Columbia?" I asked. Pictures of people chasing wild geese would be much more entertaining.

"Not that, necessarily, but we should be taking more pictures along this trip. Remember that stretch between Banff and Jasper? That was amazing. We should get some pictures of that."

"You're forgetting that we took a million pictures on the way up."

"I know, but the weather is better this time."

On the way up, we'd contended with clouds and rain, but our trip back was graced with sunshine. Mike became so enamored with the scenery along the drive that he was compelled to stop and take pictures at nearly every lookout.

"I'll just make this quick," he'd say each time, not wanting the rest of us to get annoyed that each stop prolonged our time in the car. But in his haste, he'd pull up at a lookout and jump out of the car, barely getting it in park before he did so. Leaving his door open, he'd dash out for a picture.

"You can take a little more time," I said after he returned to the car at one such stop. That particular time, he'd parked the car near the edge of a scenic overlook. "And just make sure you really have the car in park before you leave your family belted in on the edge of a cliff. I don't want us to plummet over the hill while you're getting your panoramic money shot."

"I'll try to remember," he said, which was not quite the reassurance I'd been looking for.

"It looks like tonight we'll make it to Valemount," I said, consulting a map and Trip Advisor on my phone.

"Is there a cheap hotel there?"

"There's a Super 8. It says they have 'newly renovated rooms,' which could end up meaning a new microwave in an otherwise dilapidated room."

"Nothing but the best for you, sweetie," Mike said.

"Are we going to a fancy hotel?" Ivy asked from the backseat.

"Yes," said Emilia. "Didn't you hear? It's called the Super 8."

"Wow," said Ivy. "Like superheroes."

"Yeah," Emilia confirmed. "I think it's going to be really awesome."

"Well, don't get your hopes up too high," Mike warned.

But my daughters find any hotel, no matter the condition, both super and awesome. And Mike and I were happy to find that the rooms truly were renovated, modern, clean, and comfortable, and Super 8 went up a notch in my book.

At a grocery store, we'd purchased bagged Caesar salad and a rotisserie chicken. We ate on paper plates in the Super

8 while watching the Olympics. This is a typical hotel room dinner for us, inexpensive and easy, and the type of meal and accommodations we often enjoy to offset the expenses of pricier aspects of the trip, like our stop in Banff on the way up.

"So you want to do the Radium Hot Springs?" I asked as we hit the road again the following day. While this wasn't at the top of my wish list, I knew the girls would enjoy the attraction, which we'd sped by on our way up through Canada.

"Yes, let's check it out," Mike said.

The Radium Hot Springs are nestled in a wondrous little pocket of nature, facing an imposing rock cliff. Area wildlife includes mule deer, black bears, grizzlies, mountain goats, and bighorn sheep. I found myself continually scanning the landscape to spot one of these creatures, sheep and goats being the most common on the cliff.

"This place is popular," Mike said as I paid the fee for our family of four.

"I guess we'll just meet you on the other side." We had to pass through the men's and women's locker rooms to change and shower before reaching the hot springs pools.

"Good luck," he said.

"Come on, girls, take my hands."

It's one thing to navigate narrow aisles crammed with people but an entirely different feat to do so when you're constantly in danger of brushing up against a stranger's wet and near-naked body. We carved out a tiny corner of space and changed into our bathing suits. I stashed our backpack in an empty locker.

"It's really crowded in here, Mom," Emilia said. I couldn't respond, as I was too busy mentally working through flashbacks of middle school PE classes. I took their hands, and we worked our way to the locker room exit that would lead to the pools. Showerheads sprouted from one wall alongside half a dozen signs instructing patrons to shower before entering the pools. A few women showered, while most paid no attention to the posted instructions. I stood frozen.

"Are we going, Mom?" Ivy asked.

The water from the showerhead would be cold and miserable, I was sure. But I'm an incorrigible rule follower.

"We need to shower off first," I said.

"Oh, man. Can't we just get in the pool?" Emilia pleaded.

I tried not to think about how much I hate walking barefoot on wet tiles with a hundred other barefoot, wet strangers.

"We'll just do a really quick one," I said.

"Okay." Ivy began taking off her swimsuit.

"No, Ivy, keep it on. We're not really going to shower; we're just going to get wet."

"But she took her suit off." Ivy pointed to one of the few other women in the shower. "Do I have to grow hair down there when I'm older? If I don't have to, then I don't want to."

"What's the point of getting wet here when we're about to get in a pool?" Emilia asked.

"To wash off . . . you know . . . things that might get in the pool."

The girls rolled their eyes in commiseration. We briefly dashed under lukewarm water, just enough for me to claim to have made an attempt. When the hot springs police came to round up the nonshowering criminals, I didn't want to be among them.

"All right, girls. Come on, this way," I said, herding them out of the locker room and into the springs area, where there were two giant pools.

"What took you so long?" Mike asked, likely having emerged from the men's locker room long before.

"We had to shower," I said.

"Well, you don't have to," he countered.

"There were signs posted everywhere that said you had to shower, so I had to."

He nodded then, no doubt reminding himself that he married a woman who spends way too much time worrying about doing something wrong and getting caught.

"And I'm responsible for three people," I continued. "That's three bodies, three swimsuits, and three bladders."

He put his hands up in a defensive posture and said no more.

"I'm sorry," I said. "This will be fun."

Had we more time and an unlimited budget, I would have patronized the spa on site. Mike and the girls could enjoy the springs while I received a hot stone massage and an organic seaweed body wrap. I have no idea what an organic seaweed body wrap is, but I'm a big fan of sushi, so I'm pretty sure that makes me the ideal candidate.

Instead, we bobbed around the serene hot pool for a bit, then made our way over to the warm pool, which had deeper areas and where kids could swim and splash about. I didn't see any mountain man cooties in either pool. The girls enjoyed themselves, and I realized that while the springs were not as wonderful as Mike had hoped, likely due to the crowds and lack of poolside beverages, they were also not as awful as I had feared.

* * *

"This is an odd little room," I muttered to Mike as we waited to check in to the Motel Tyrol. "I can't tell if it's a reception area or living room."

To the right of the reception desk were stairs leading up, and at the base of the stairs was a pile of shoes and jackets. Was this more of a B&B? Would we be asked to add our own shoes and jackets to the pile and then be shown to a room upstairs? If so, I was ready to bolt.

"I think maybe the owners live upstairs," he whispered. "I don't know. It's weird."

Mike began the check-in process while I eyed an obese corgi, a living pile of mushy dog that took up residence near the mound of shoes and jackets. Poorly taxidermied fish, birds, and a deer decorated the walls. Maybe the taxidermist had done a fine job, and all mounted animals looked like the unfortunate creatures decorating the walls of the Motel Tyrol reception area. The problem could have been that they were displayed too low on the walls, giving me a much closer view of them, in all their gory glory, than I wanted to see.

Luckily, we weren't directed up the stairs but instead drove around the back of the building, where doors from the parking lot led into the individual rooms.

"I'm kind of afraid of what we're going to find in there," I admitted.

"I'm sure it will be fine," Mike said. "If we can ever get in."

The parking lot was narrow and required an eighteen-point turn to get our truck into its designated space. Inside we found an odd but not displeasing room with an intense green carpet and white linoleum counters veined with streaks of faux gold.

"This place is amazing," Emilia said. "It's so fancy!"

"Look at the pretty green carpet," Ivy added.

"First the Super 8 and now this! We are living the life."

* * *

Bad Company

I'm still living the life where you get home and open the fridge and there's half a pot of yogurt and a half a can of flat Coca-Cola.

—Alan Rickman

"If we really book it, we can make it back a day early," Mike said. "We'd save the cost of another hotel room." The thought of not having to spend as much and having our own bed and kitchen was alluring.

"Besides, there's no way we could top back-to-back nights in the Super 8 and the Motel Tyrol," I added, hoping to keep the girls thinking that we'd stayed in two luxurious hotels. "But we'll have to cancel the cleaners."

We afforded renting the home on the island in part by renting out our own home during our absence. By coming home a day early, we were cutting off the time that we had allotted for a cleaning company to come in and set the home right again before our return.

"That's okay," Mike said. "I'll help, and we'll just know

that as soon as we get home, we'll have some cleaning to do. Besides, maybe these renters will be really clean people."

"They have six kids," I reminded him.

"Right."

"But I guess if we just expect the worst and prepare ourselves for a few hours of cleaning, it will be okay."

"Emilia?" Ivy said to her sister in the backseat. "Yesterday you said that today we could talk."

The day prior during a long drive, Emilia had tired of her sister's inquiries and in her exasperation promised Ivy that they would talk tomorrow. I recognized that Emilia came up with this plan after years of hearing it from me. "Maybe tomorrow" was an appropriate response to any number of requests from children.

"Can we go to the zoo?"

"Maybe tomorrow."

"Can I have a treat?"

"You can have one tomorrow."

"How do babies get made?"

"Ask me tomorrow."

It's not that I want to keep my kids from fun activities; they have plenty of treats, and I don't try to put off telling them the facts of life; but like most parents, I often grow weary of the endless stream of inquiries and unfortunately and routinely default to tomorrow. It's a parental form of procrastination.

"Fine, Ivy." Emilia's annoyance was poorly masked. "What do you want to talk about?"

"I don't know," said Ivy. "What do you want to talk about?" This is typical of Ivy. She wants interaction and doesn't much care what the topic is.

"Hmm, let me think," Emilia said. "What about a

discussion of our favorite *Mary Poppins* characters?"

Ivy was agreeable to this, and the two proceeded to dissect the *Mary Poppins* cast with arguments for and against different characters. They were debating the probability of marriage between Burt and Mary when we pulled into the Winchester Wolf Research Center. It was the final stop to break up the long drive before completing the journey home. I wanted to write an article on the center, in part because it's fascinating to have a Wolf Research Center in Idaho, where you'll see a substantial number of bumper stickers that read, "Wolves, smoke a pack day," along with a picture of a target or gun or dead wolf or something else to communicate how much the driver would really like to kill some wolves. It's political and polarizing in the Pacific Northwest. Naturally, I wanted to learn more.

The research center was manned by a young intern named Danaé. She was passionate about her work and good at presenting both sides of the wolf debate, though one need only stand in the center for a moment to realize that the intent was to preserve a healthy wolf population, not wipe them out.

"So, if you're an intern, where do you stay?" I asked. "Do they put you up in an apartment in town or something?"

"Town" might have been overkill for the sparse signs of residential and commercial activity we'd seen leading into the center, though we did pass through the beautifully maintained campground of Winchester State Park.

"Oh no, not an apartment," Danaé answered. "The interns all stay in tents in the campground."

"Well, how long do you intern for?" Mike asked.

"Three months," she replied, then turned back to the girls to tell them about wolf conservation.

"Three months in a tent," Mike whispered.

"Oh, to be young," I said.

"Mom, can we please get something here?" Emilia asked. "We never did pick out our Alaska souvenirs."

I realized she was right. I'd promised each of them the chance to choose a souvenir before we departed the Last Frontier, but that promise (like so many tomorrows) had gone by the wayside.

"Yes, you can pick something," I said, then quickly added the qualifier, "depending on what it is and how much it costs."

Emilia picked out prints of some of the wolves that had lived at the research center in a protected area of land. She'd later scavenge through our house, find a family photo in the right-sized frame, and cover our memories and smiling faces with a wolf picture.

"I choose this," Ivy said, holding up a stuffed animal.

"Black bear. Good choice, Ivy," Emilia said, "though you already have a *lot* of stuffed animals."

"Are you going to name him?" Danaé asked.

"I already did. His name is Balloon."

"Baloo? Just like in *The Jungle Book*? That's a great name!"

"No, Bal*loon*," Ivy corrected.

"Oh," said Danaé. "Well, that's a good name, too."

We thanked Danaé for her effort, enthusiasm, and knowledge and headed back to the truck.

"You know, I have to use the bathroom really quick," I said to Mike. "You guys get in the truck, and I'll be right there."

Mike eyed the outhouse that stood along the wooden pathway suspiciously. "Good luck with that," he said.

I wasn't thrilled about using an outhouse, but the only other facilities nearby were at the campground, which surely wouldn't be much better, and I really had to pee. I opened the bathroom door, preparing to have multiple senses assaulted, and instead found the cleanest bathroom I'd ever seen. It was pristine and odorless. Placards on the walls told the story of the bathroom, which had been constructed from soybeans and recycled materials including fibers, grocery bags, and pallets. Waste was composted with wood chips. Rainwater was used for bathroom cleanings. I felt like I'd walked into a tree hugger's church, and part of me never wanted to leave. I've never felt that way about a bathroom, before or since. Our parting was bittersweet.

"Maybe our house won't be bad at all," Mike said as we pulled onto our road.

"I don't know," I said. "It's not just the six kids that worries me. In my last e-mail correspondence with the renter, he wanted to know how much of a cleaning fee he'd paid as part of the rental."

"Why is that a bad thing?" Mike asked.

"Because it was almost like he was calculating how much of a mess he felt he could leave us. Like paying the cleaning fee entitled his family to trash the place."

"I'm sure that's not the case," Mike said.

Five minutes later, we walked into the *Twilight Zone* version of our once-habitable home.

"Dear lord, it's awful," I said.

"Kids, go play outside," Mike instructed. "Mommy and I have some work to do."

"Can't we just watch a movie?" Emilia asked.

"Yes," we said in unison, buckling immediately.

The following few days included searching for the laundry basket, which had been relocated to the backyard and was home to a large arachnid, and trying to locate the coffee maker, which was hidden high in our booze cabinet.

"Apparently caffeine is as offensive as our tequila," I said.

"There's candy embedded in the rug," Mike noted.

"They left us with five pounds of sugar," I said.

When I eventually checked our downstairs bathroom, I found the mirror coated in a thick layer of hand soap. We could only deduce that they'd instructed a young child to clean the mirror, and said child had thought that smearing soap over the mirror was the best way to go about such a task.

Every sheet and towel in our home sat in a giant mountain of soiled fabric on our basement floor. We washed load after load, discovering with the first one that they hadn't cleaned out the lint filter in the weeks they'd stayed there. It was a wonder the house hadn't burned to the ground. Whenever we'd discover a new domestic atrocity, I'd struggle not to mutter, *"Fucking renters!"*

After a week, I thought we had everything back in place. We ordered a new washing machine, as ours had conked out entirely (fucking renters), and cleaned up substantial cat litter, as our renters had casually ignored our no-pet policy.

We pulled into the garage, having taken the girls out for pizza. Along one wall of the garage was a trashcan in which I kept pruning shears and other gardening tools, along with a sign taped over the top of it that read, "This is NOT a trash can." I'd put the sign in place for the benefit of Mike's parents, who routinely used it to discard their mail. But I'd hoped it would serve a similar purpose for the renters. I peered in to see our gardening implements caked with half-eaten, melted Popsicles and draped in wrappers from ice-cream sandwiches. The girls were getting out of the truck, and when they weren't looking, I mouthed to Mike, "Those *fucking* renters!"

"Everything's going to be okay, honey," he said. "Take a deep breath."

"I hate renters," I said. "I don't want to rent the house anymore." We've had good renters and bad renters during our travels over the years, but these particular renters had been the hardest on our home.

"You know you'd still do it again if it came down to it," he said. "Yes, it's a pain in the butt, but it's also worth the adventure. It makes this whole way of life possible."

I began the sticky task of cleaning out the bin and bit my tongue from telling Mike that I hate it when he's right.

* * *

My First Gay Bachelor Party

The only kind of seafood I trust is the fish stick, a totally featureless fish that doesn't have eyeballs or fins.

—Dave Barry

One year after our Alaskan adventure, Mike and I had a rare opportunity to travel without kids. We had a gay bachelor party to attend in Ketchikan. I'm not saying that my daughters weren't *ready* to attend their first gay bachelor party, they absolutely were, but my mother had recently moved to Boise and was available to watch the girls while Mike and I made the quick trip. I had also come off of five consecutive months of full-time homeschooling and, at the risk of losing my Mother of the Year award, the prospect of a few days away sounded like an AMAZING AND FANTASTIC IDEA.

I wasn't the only female attending the gay bachelor party. It was organized by Levi, whose wife, Jen (my favorite Australian), was there as well. Levi was best man to Groom #2. (I'm sure our friend Chris would much rather be Groom

#1, because who doesn't want to be #1? And because #2 makes people think of poop. Sorry, Chris. Since Chad proposed to you, he gets to be Groom #1. If you wanted to be Groom #1 that badly, you should have proposed first, but you were probably too busy flexing in the mirror.) While Levi, Jen, Mike, and I thought of the event as a gay bachelor party, I'm sure Chris and Chad thought of it as a weekend with their nerdy straight friends. The fact that wives were included, and that no one other than the Groom and Groom were gay, takes it down a notch from being a true gay bachelor party. In any case, I thanked both Chris and Chad for letting Jen and me (and our vaginas) be a part of the event.

The first thing that greeted us as we entered Ketchikan's tiny airport was a stuffed mountain goat in a glass case. It was positioned so that as I emerged from the hallway connecting the plane to the terminal, there it was staring directly at me. We passed the goat and headed for the stairs down to the exit.

"Oh, wait," said Mike. "I want to change my shoes."

"Right now? In the airport?"

"I don't get to wear these that often," said Mike, pulling his classic brown, big-ass, rubber Xtratuf boots from one of our bags. "And we're in Alaska, so I'm wearing them."

"I guess it does look pretty rainy out," I agreed, and swapped my tennis shoes for the hiking boots I'd brought. We packed light, without checking any luggage, but sturdy, spare footwear was a must.

"Wow, that thing is huge." I motioned to a giant elk head mounted on the wall in the stairwell.

"That's a Roosevelt bull. They can get to be over a thousand pounds," Mike said. "The funny thing is they don't even have elk in Ketchikan." It's pretty amazing to think that an animal that survives mainly on grasses, berries, mushrooms, and lichen can grow to such massive proportions, and in my mind, this is proof enough that going on a diet would be futile. We left the airport and waited for a ferry to shuttle us across the Tongass Narrows to the actual town of Ketchikan. When the ferry arrived, Levi walked up the gangway to greet us.

"Welcome! I'm so glad you guys could come," he said. "We've got some really fun stuff planned for this weekend." Levi spoke of fishing and visiting nearby fjords as the ferry made its short journey across the water. The fjord visit would be by floatplane to Misty Fjords, a national monument and wilderness area forty miles east of Ketchikan. While we'd all find the fjords beautiful, Jen would spend the plane ride there hunched over a barf bag while I suffered a full-blown and entirely unexpected panic attack (my first). Still, the pictures would be amazing.

"The forecast doesn't look too good while we're here, right?" asked Mike.

"No, no it doesn't. But that's Alaska for you."

"Well," I said. "I guess you can't have rainbows without a little rain."

Compared to Sitka, Ketchikan appears far more industrial. Along with cruise ships and marinas, the land bordering the Narrows is home to shipping containers and heavy equipment, which I'm sure does really important and manly things. Also of note is that Ketchikan is located on Revillagigedo Island, so named in the late 1700s by Captain George Vancouver, who apparently liked to screw with people by bestowing names nearly impossible to pronounce. Ketchikan also has the world's largest collection of standing totem poles, some of which we saw as Levi drove south along Tongass Avenue, briefly through downtown, then beyond it and toward his home. Levi and Jen live most of the year at their home in Australia but maintain a home in Ketchikan as well.

The drive was a good snapshot of Alaskan life. Immense, beautifully maintained waterfront homes sat beside crumbling structures and dilapidated trailers. Residents of the Lower 48 tend to romanticize Alaska, but as with anywhere, the reality, continually battered by harsh elements, doesn't always match the postcard.

"Levi, I keep seeing these waterfalls everywhere, with water just gushing down." On one side of the road was the town, backed by mountains; the waterway flanked the road on the other side. "Is that just because of spring? Runoff from snow melting in the mountains?" I asked.

"It's snowmelt and rain," he answered, "but that's not just in spring. It pretty much does that year round."

I eyed Mike's Xtratufs with envy.

"So we took the guys to a logging show this morning," Levi said. "That was pretty fun."

"I'm sorry we missed it," I said. "What the heck do they do at a logging show? Is there a lot of flexing and chainsaws?"

"Exactly. And red plaid flannel shirts and suspenders. But tomorrow we'll go king salmon fishing, and that should be a lot of fun, too."

In Levi and Jen's kitchen, I'd later come across the program from the Great Alaskan Lumberjack Show, which promised "Rugged Woodsmen and a Rowdy Good Time." These weren't Alaskan lumberjacks but traveling lumberjacks, hailing from all over the United States and including one woman. They competed in log rolling and ax throwing and other such lumberjack arts.

We hadn't seen Chris, aka Groom #2, in over a decade. It was a joyful reunion during which Chris insisted that we looked exactly the same as we had a decade prior, which was a bald-faced lie. While Mike and I (okay, especially me) had grown softer and outward, Chris had focused on perfecting his physique and developing a protein shake addiction. We met Chad, aka Groom #1 and also physically perfect, for the first time and congratulated them both on their impending nuptials, then settled in to drinking wine and chatting through the afternoon.

"I think I'm going to make an apple pie," said Chris.

"Just like that?" I questioned. "You're just going to whip up an apple pie? From scratch?"

"Sure! Why not?"

While Chris set about making pie, we talked about the evolution of the bachelor party. For people in their twenties, bachelor and bachelorette parties might involve various degrees of debauchery, things never to be mentioned after the night in question. Though Mike and I married young, we didn't have scandalous parties. I had a surprise get-together at a bar, where women gave me cooking gadgets, because word had spread that I was so inept in the kitchen that it might actually endanger my marriage. I remember them trying to explain to me how to use a garlic press and what a steamer basket might steam. Mike had no party whatsoever. He had plenty of friends, but they were all twenty and twenty-one years old at the time. None of them had the resources or wherewithal to pull a party together.

Levi married in his thirties, and Chris recounted organizing his bachelor weekend, which was a two-day rafting trip down the South Fork of the American River in Northern California.

"I remember waking up covered in daddy longlegs," said Chris.

"I remember everyone acting tough on the river until we hit the white water, and then suddenly we're all huddled in the middle of the boat clinging to each other," said Mike.

"I remember Jack Daniels," added Levi.

"And here I am baking pie," said Chris. "This is forty."

"Want me to take your picture?" I asked.

"Of course I do," said Chris. "Make sure my arms look amazing."

"Why don't you take off your shirt and put the apron back on and then I'll take it," I suggested.

"That's good thinking."

"Stop inflating his ego," chided Chad.

"I'm not," I protested. "I'm exploiting it."

At some point, the conversation turned to tattoos.

"Amanda has a new one," Mike volunteered. "She's got lower-back action. But she's still a nerd. It's a tattoo of the word 'Literary.'"

"I felt the need to forever commemorate my love of all things book related."

"Let's see it!" Chris demanded.

"No," I declined. Had I shared Chris and Chad's extremely low body-fat percentage, I might have. "It's less of a tramp stamp now and more of a . . . muffin-top accentuater."

"Are you guys excited about fishing tomorrow?" Mike asked.

In a complete deadpan monotone, Chad replied, "So. Excited."

"I wouldn't say we're *not* outdoorsy," Chris confided. "I mean, I love to drink rosé on the deck. That counts, right?"

"We're just not Levi-level outdoorsy," Chad added.

Jen laughed knowingly. "*Most* people aren't Levi-level outdoorsy."

"I know exactly what you mean," I said. "Anytime Levi says something is just a short walk . . ."

"It ends up being five miles," said Chris. "We call it the Levi mile."

"But tomorrow should be fun," said Chad. "We get to go out on a boat. I'm sure we'll have a good time."

* * *

"I'm so cold," said Chris.

"My feet feel like ice," I muttered through chattering teeth.

Per Levi's instructions, we'd been ready to depart promptly at 7 a.m. It was windy, cold, and rainy as Levi's friend Kit took us king salmon fishing on his boat. Jen had stayed behind with kids while I joined the guys for the day's adventure.

"Why didn't we bring coffee?" Mike asked.

"With booze in it," I added.

"Yeah, we're doing this all wrong," said Chris. "Fishing is *always* supposed to involve alcohol. That's just a given."

"We got one on the line," called Levi. "Who's going to reel it in?"

Chris momentarily forgot about our lack of alcohol and sprang to action. Despite his claims of being a rosé-all-day type of outdoorsman, Chris had attended the California Maritime Academy with Levi and Mike, where the three rowed crew together. He's familiar with boats and hard work.

"That's a nice one," said Kit as he netted the fish, a

decent-sized king salmon. "We got another one on this line." Four poles trailed lines from the stern, and it was not uncommon to have more than one fish hooked at a time.

"Chad, you're up!" yelled Levi. Chad dutifully took the pole and reeled in the line, but the fish was too small and had to be thrown back.

Kit used the gaff hook to free the fish, and I called, "Sorry!" to it as it swam away. Chad and I retreated to the wheelhouse to escape the rain and wind.

"I really hope they don't call me to action again," he said.

"I think you paid your dues," I replied.

When the rain stopped for a time and the sky brightened, we emerged from the wheelhouse to the boat's back deck. I watched Kit bait the hooks, placing what looked like a little plastic fish helmet over a small baitfish and securing it in place with a toothpick fragment. The toothpick went through small holes in the fish helmet, which I'm pretty sure is not actually called a fish helmet, and through the head of the bait.

The guys took their turns reeling in fish, but aside from Chris's catch, the others hooked were all too small to keep. When it was my turn to reel in a fish, my three minutes with rod in hand felt like an epic battle of woman versus beast. I felt vindicated when we discovered that it was a twenty-pound fish and our future dinner. And despite my squeamishness with the killing of land animals, I gleefully posed for pictures holding up the salmon as it dripped blood onto my shoes.

The rain picked up again, and Chad and I returned to the wheelhouse while Mike, Levi, and Chris took turns trying to catch another big one. "I hope they get more fish," I said. "I really do. They're just not allowed to be bigger than mine."

Chad replied, without a moment's hesitation, "That's my

rule when dating."

Hours passed, and the cold chilled us thoroughly before we thankfully headed back to the marina. Kit expertly fileted our two salmon, and we descended upon the small general store to buy doughnuts, coffee, and Baileys with which to spike it.

"Kit, come have a doughnut," Chris called.

We chatted and enjoyed the warmth of coffee and booze before thanking Kit and heading to Levi's truck in the parking lot.

"Did you see Kit eat that doughnut with his bloody fingers?" Chad asked. "Oh my god."

"Hey, look over there," Chris demanded. "This really *is* a gay bachelor party." He pointed to the distant sky over the water. The rain ceased, and the sun shone in its place, yielding a perfect, Alaskan, gay-bachelor-party rainbow.

For a moment I forgot that we were traveling without Emilia and Ivy, and my instinct was to point out the rainbow to my daughters. While adults might stop to appreciate the beauty of a rainbow, it's far more impactful to children. I remember my nine-year-old self, wanting to challenge any adult who told me I wouldn't be able to find the rainbow's end, imagining an adventure across miles of farmland. There were no leprechauns or cauldrons of gold coins in my fantasy, but there would be a clearing of grass and clover, and I'd find myself basking in a mist of colors where the rainbow touched the earth. Maybe my daughters had similar fancies; I wished they were there so I could find out.

I spent the rest of the day consumed with thoughts of where the four of us might still journey, where circumstance or happenstance would lead us. It's cliché but true, how kids quickly grow, how time speeds up with each passing year, regardless of how we feel about it. As the ages and stages fly by, no matter how fast, we'll continue to see the world along the way.

* * *

Acknowledgments

Thank you, Jim Barron, Tom Reale, Charlie and Karen Haley, Michael Colliver and Melissa Haley, Mary-Lou Colliver, Phyllis Hackett, Dylan Haley and Ashley Norman, Mark Hackett, Levi and Jennifer Benedict, Chris Walker and Chad Everett, Elizabeth Day, Ross Patty, Sarah Tregay, Mike and Jan Turner, Jared Cozby, Corinne Danzl, and anyone who had to deal with me during this trip. Thanks to all readers, Alaskans, Canadians, and the few hippie holdouts in Northern Idaho. Thanks to Rick Just and all of the friends at Idaho State Parks. Above all, thanks to Ivy, Emilia, and Mike—you are my favorite people. This would be so boring without you.

If you enjoyed this book, please consider posting a review online.

Follow AK Turner and Vagabonding with Kids at:
VagabondingWithKids.com
AKTurner.com
Facebook.com/VagabondingWithKids
Facebook.com/AKTurnerAuthor
Twitter.com/VagabondingKids
Pinterest.com/VagabondKids
Instagram.com/VagabondingWithKids

Listen to Emilia's "Girl Around the World" podcast at:
EmiliaTurner.com

Epigraph Sources

Chapter 1, "Scat": William S. Burroughs.

Chapter 2, "Onward": George Carlin.

Chapter 3, "O Canada": Joel Madden, https://www.brainyquote.com/quotes/quotes/j/joelmadden219161.html.

Chapter 4, "Don't Forget the Bear Spray": "Be Bear Aware," Center for Wildlife Information, accessed October 21, 2016, http://www.centerforwildlifeinformation.org/BeBearAware/BearSpray/bearspray.html.

Chapter 5, "*Matanuska*": Alaska Trekker, accessed October 29, 2016, http://alaskatrekker.com/planning-trip/alaska-marine-highway/.

Chapter 6, "Island Life": Emily van Lidth de Jeude, "Wild Food: Killing Our Own Meat," Rickshaw Unschooling, accessed November 8, 2016, http://rickshawunschooling.blogspot.ca/2007/10/wild-food-killing-our-own-meat.html.

Chapter 7, "*Zarina*": Kenneth Grahame, *The Wind in the Willows*.

Chapter 8, "Fish Slayer": Dave Barry.

Chapter 9, "Magic Island": David Sedaris, "Ask the Author Live: David Sedaris," *New Yorker*, accessed January 17, 2017, http://www.newyorker.com/books/ask-the-author/ask-the-author-live-david-sedaris.

Chapter 10, "New Archangel Dancers": "Culture & History," Sitka Convention & Visitors Bureau, accessed January 24, 2017, http://

www.sitka.org/explore/culture-history/.

Chapter 11, "Birds of Prey": "Frequently Asked Questions," Alaska Raptor Center, accessed January 27, 2017, https://alaskaraptor.org/faq/.

Chapter 12, "I Do": *The Princess Bride*, directed by Rob Reiner (Act III Communications, Buttercup Films, Ltd., The Princess Bride, Ltd., 1987), accessed January 27, 2017, http://www.imdb.com/title/tt0093779/quotes.

Chapter 13, "Battle of the Bilge": James Joyce, *Ulysses*.

Chapter 14, "Skookum": Derek Walcott.

Chapter 15, "Crapshooters and Hot Box Girls": Charlie Chaplin.

Chapter 16, "Parental Duties": Paula Ann Solis, "NOAA Still Chasing Entangled Whale in Southeast," Juneau Empire, accessed February 13, 2017, http://juneauempire.com/local/2016-06-06/noaa-still-chasing-entangled-whale-southeast.

Chapter 17, "Russian Girl": Lucille Ball.

Chapter 18, "Theft of Daylight": "Tlingit Fact Sheet," Native Languages, accessed February 22, 2017, http://www.bigorrin.org/tlingit_kids.htm.

Chapter 19, "Fortress of the Bear": Bill Bryson, *A Walk in the Woods*.

Chapter 20, "Porky, Bishop Innocent, and the Heckler": Sarah Vowell.

Chapter 21, "Reunion": Paul Simon.

Chapter 22, "Bathing with Strangers": Britney Spears, CNN Travel, accessed March 10, 2017, http://travel.cnn.com/explorations/life/20-funniest-things-ever-said-about-travel-015440/.

Chapter 23, "Bad Company": Alan Rickman.

Chapter 24, "My First Gay Bachelor Party": Dave Barry.

Endnotes

1   James Baichtal, "The Buried Forest of Alaska's Kruzof Island: a Window into the Past," United States Department of Agriculture, March 7, 2014, accessed October 24, 2016, http://blogs.usda.gov/2014/03/07/the-buried-forest-of-alaskas-kruzof-island-a-window-into-the-past/.

2   https://www.nps.gov/glba/planyourvisit/ak-state-ferry-to-gustavus.htm.

3   Brielle Schaeffer, "Sea lion harasses Sitka fisherman in harbor," KTOO Public Media, May 17, 2016, accessed November 9, 2016, http://www.ktoo.org/2016/05/17/sea-lion-harasses-sitka-fisherman-harbor/.

4   Cornell Lab of Ornithology, "Bald Eagle, Life History, All About Birds," accessed December 6, 2016, https://www.allaboutbirds.org/guide/bald_eagle/lifehistory.

5   https://oca.org/holy-synod/bishops/the-most-blessed-theodosius.

6   https://rainfall.weatherdb.com/.

7   https://www.currentresults.com/Weather/US/average-annual-precipitation-by-city.php.

8   http://members.home.nl/t.overberg1/Totem_Pole.htm#Low.